**TERRY FARRELL**
Interiors and the Legacy
of Postmodernism

TERRY FARRELL
Interiors and the Legacy
of Postmodernism

# TERRY FARRELL
# Interiors and
# the Legacy of
# Postmodernism

Laurence King Publishing

**LAURENCE KING**

Published in 2011 by Laurence King
Publishing Ltd
361-373 City Road
London EC1V 1LR
United Kingdom
Tel: +44 20 7841 6900
Fax: +44 20 7841 6910
e-mail: enquiries@laurenceking.com
www.laurenceking.com

Published in 2011 by
Laurence King Publishing Ltd

ISBN: 978-1-85669-822-1
Design: Godfrey Design
Senior editor: Peter Jones
Printed in Italy

Previous pages: Staircase, The Royal
Institution, Piccadilly

Contents

'For all its contradictions and occasional absurdities, it is clear that Postmodernism has remade the world in ways that can never be retracted.'

Eleanor Heartney

Sir Terry Farrell CBE was born in Manchester but grew up in Newcastle Upon Tyne where he went to university. He then went on to graduate with a Masters in city planning from the University of Pennsylvania and returned to London where he has lived ever since. Terry founded his practice in 1965 and has continued it in his sole name since 1980. His offices in London and Hong Kong have both delivered major award-winning projects.

He is qualified as both a town planner and an architect and is currently Visiting Professor at The Bartlett, University College London. He has taught at various universities from Cambridge to the Architectural Association and the University of Pennsylvania. His completed buildings in the UK include MI6, Charing Cross (Embankment Place),

the new Home Office building and The Deep in Hull. Large-scale infrastructure planning and buildings dominate his work in the Far East, which includes Incheon Airport Transportation Building in Korea and Beijing South and Guangzhou high-speed rail stations in China. His masterplanning work in the UK includes the Quayside in Newcastle, Brindley Place in Birmingham as well as Greenwich Peninsula and Earls Court in London; in Hong Kong his office built the West Kowloon station masterplan – still the largest air rights development of its kind in the world.

Terry was an English Heritage commissioner and has worked with many city governments as an advisor on strategic affairs – which includes the role of Design Champion for Edinburgh, board member of City Development Company of

Gateshead and Newcastle, and central government advisor and Design Champion for the Thames Gateway. He currently sits on the Mayor of London's Design Advisory Panel and Outer London Commission. He has won many awards, and his many books include *Shaping London: The Patterns and Forms that Make the Metropolis* (2009). In 1996 he was awarded a CBE and in 2001 a knighthood.

# Interiors as Small Cities

**Terry Farrell**

The idea, and then the timing, for this book came originally from the V&A holding the UK's first review of Postmodernism for two decades, in September 2011. My first thought was to write and advocate that any review should be as wide in its perspective as possible – to expand to city, place, architecture, design and interiors and relate these to all the modern-era arts – theatre, film, literature, innovative painting, installations and so on, a maximalist reaction to an age of reductivist limitation.

In the end I started this book with a much narrower field – namely interiors – and then let it grow outwards. Partly I felt the aim and ambition would otherwise be too wide to handle. Postmodernism was all-encompassing, not a style but an era, and as a phenomenon it was about holistic connectivity, the broadening of all viewpoints. Such a task as originally envisioned would have been so wide and all-encompassing that eventually it would have been self-defeating. So I settled on interiors, as connectivity could be explored from the smallest scale and then expand. In this way, Alberti's observation would be the book's best thematic guide 'the city is like some large house, and the house is in turn like some small city'.

The book deals with not only continuums of scale but also those of time, of changing past uses, particularities of context and their history, and how nothing is ever really 'finished'. Self-ordering and organic responses to life's 'chaos' are embraced and expressed (see particularly architects' offices and family homes). I have included just three types of interiors – homes, museums and workplaces – with a limited number of projects, but these range in time over three decades to help show continuity and legacy.

The book, as it was accompanying an exhibition, ended up in the main part as something of a picture book. But the idea had evolved to invite essay responses from others, and since I'm involved in teaching at the University College London, conversations began that eventually ended up with two such essays being added to the book. As I wrote in emails to Colin Fournier and Tim Makower, the authors of these essays, when the book was underway, the result is a kind of assemblage. In a sort of Postmodernist collage I like to think, the threads are there to be drawn in several ways, in different directions and into different readings. And what is more, it was so stimulating and such fun for all of us involved, celebrating together the cultural event of this review of the Postmodern age.

Robert Venturi's book *Complexity and Contradiction in Architecture* has been, for decades, the defining source, the nearest to what might be loosely called a 'manifesto of Postmodernism' and in my view nothing has replaced it. But I believe the essay Colin Fournier has written for this book changes this view: here is an up-to-date positional text with a high level of seriousness, fairness and perception. I really do think that with or without this volume, which almost incidentally was its catalyst, Colin's essay stands as a definitive landmark in the contemporary discussion of Postmodernism. The essay itself is a fitting legacy to an important cultural phenomenon.

Tim Makower, before he began his essay for the book, commented 'I'm not sure about Postmodern architecture but I really am convinced of the legacy of Postmodern urban planning.' My own career since the early 1980s has moved more and more towards urban issues and city planning, and Tim gives passionate voice to so much that I too hold of greatest value today. Tim has taken as his guide the above quotation from Alberti on cities and houses and the scale continuum. I am indebted to him for a learned, timely and insightful view of narrative and city-making.

My thanks to Philip Cooper and his colleagues at Laurence King for taking on a bit of a mixture of a book. The book was very much a late idea and it therefore could only be made with something of a *jeu d'esprit*. It demanded a lot of photo research, assembly and managing, and our Emma Davies did all this and more to get it done. Her organizational skills have held it all together. Thanks to Jo Evans and Jess Crook for typing the manuscript and Hannah Smart for some of the sketches. Rebecca Holmes skilfully worked on the design and layout with the book's designer Jason Godfrey, and last but not least Graciela Moreno who teaches at the Bartlett led on integrating the essays by Colin and Tim, as well as writing the project descriptions and working with Hannah Smart on the sketches for the book. I am grateful to her for her extraordinary energy and enthusiasm for a project she didn't even know existed a very short time ago.

Of course there are many whose work lies behind the pictures and designs shown – photographers, architects, designers. These are acknowledged at length on page 188 of the book, but it almost goes without saying that it is to these very creative people, who work within or with our practice past and present, that the fullest credit is due: without them there would be nothing to show or write about – no book at all!

'I am for richness of meaning rather than clarity of meaning; for the implicit function as well as the explicit function. I prefer "both-and" to "either-or," black and white, and sometimes gray, to black or white. A valid architecture evokes many levels of meaning and combinations of focus: its space and its elements become readable and workable in several ways at once.

But an architecture of complexity and contradiction has a special obligation toward the whole: its truth must be in its totality or its implications of totality. It must embody the difficult unity of inclusion rather than the easy unity of exclusion. More is not less.'

Robert Venturi, *Complexity and Contradiction in Architecture*,1966

Professor Colin Fournier was born in 1944, is of Franco-British origin and was educated at the Architectural Association in London. He is Professor of Architecture and Urbanism at the Bartlett School of Architecture, University College London (UCL) where he is Director of the Master of Architecture Course in Urban Design (MArch UD) as well as Director of one of the Architecture Diploma Units.

An architect and planner in private practice, Colin is based in London. His interests and professional activities are split equally between architecture and urbanism. He was an associate member of the famous experimental design group Archigram Architects and was for many years the Planning Director of the Ralph M. Parsons Company in Pasadena, California, US, in which capacity he has designed and implemented a number of major new town projects in the Middle East, in particular the town of Yanbu in Saudi Arabia.

Colin subsequently worked in partnership with Bernard Tschumi on the planning and design of the Parc de la VIllette in Paris. He is, together with his partner Sir Peter Cook, the co-author of the Graz Kunsthaus, a radical museum of modern art in the city of Graz, Austria, that was completed in 2003 and has received a considerable amount of international recognition. The Austrian Goldener Ehrenzeichen medal was awarded to him in 2005 by the Governor of Styria for his role in this project as Partner in Charge. In collaboration with co-authors Professor Volker Giencke and Petra Friedl he has recently won an international competition for a major residential extension of the town of Riga, capital of Latvia.

# The Legacy of Postmodernism

Professor Colin Fournier

The change of zeitgeist that became known as 'Postmodernism' was one in which architecture played a dominant role, just as it did in Modernism, because of the highly noticeable design changes that took place in the built environment.

But Postmodernism was not a style: it was a period of profound changes that affected all aspects of our culture, not just architecture. It was a powerful reaction against what was then the universally established mindset of Modernism – its over-prescriptive 'meta-narratives', as Jean-Francois Lyotard labelled them in *La Condition Postmoderne*.

It was a spectacular return, at the beginning of post-industrial society, of all that had been repressed for several decades, a re-emergence of philosophical concepts, intellectual, political and artistic positions that had been held at bay, almost universally and for far too long, under the hegemony of the previous regime.

This reaction was profound and led to irreversible changes. The radical legacy of Postmodernism does not lie in the traces that it has left in terms of the surface appearance of the architectural object, traces that many of us, coming from a Modernist tradition, found at times profoundly irritating: it lies in the shift of our perception of the world as we moved from the machine age, and its dominant modes of production, to the information age. It emancipated our knowledge and our ways of acting within this new world.

These changes have affected many disciplines other than architecture and they are still taking place. It is not yet clear how they will evolve from here on, but it is clear that there is no way back to the orthodoxy of Modernism, for the changes have had a deep impact on the most fundamental components of architecture and urbanism: our conception of space, time and meaning.

## Space

Modernism imposed a reductivist perception of space. It saw space as the ideal, homogeneous, an isomorphic grid of Euclidean geometry, spreading ad infinitum. That was the undifferentiated abstract milieu within which any new architecture had to be seen to be inserted (in lieu of a contextual understanding of its specific location within actual geographic and urban space); it was also the stuff, the pre-ordered geometric mould, out of which the architectural object had to be formed, as well as its interior spaces and even its furniture, down to the smallest accessories, in a holistic 'Gesamkunstwerk' delirium hardly ever before experienced in history.

Strangely, there was nothing 'modern' about this conception of space. It was not informed by the extraordinary scientific discoveries of the time: neither by the warped space of Einstein's relativity, nor by the possibly even stranger geometries put forward by rogue mathematicians such as Riemann or Lobachevsky, nor by the more contemporary explorations into the theory of complexity -- Benoît Mandelbrot's fractals or chaos theory, which one would have thought would be highly influential on a movement claiming from the start to embody *l'esprit nouveau*. It was nothing but the stable, rectilinear, familiar, universal space of the Enlightenment, dating back to Newton and, further back, to Euclid.

Postmodernism challenged this philosophically antiquated and limited understanding of the structure of space and reintroduced the notion that there are indeed many different structures of space, not only theoretically but also empirically, as is evident from any sympathetic observation of the world around us. It emphasized the uniqueness and significance of 'place', i.e. the singularity and specificity of space and therefore its inherent diversity and complexity. It rehabilitated the socio-anthropological evidence that there are different kinds of spaces constructed by different people, different cultures, for different purposes, in different parts of the world but also co-evolving within the same city. It rejected the unconsciously neocolonial ideology of Modernism and stressed that these diverse spaces have equal value, pointing out that they can (and do) coexist side by side, that space can legitimately be heterogeneous, multilayered, pluralist, eclectic, at times even disordered, 'deconstructed', uncontrolled, chaotic, messy, unplanned, alien, monstrous.

Most significantly, following Colin Rowe's seminal *Collage City*, a book that, together with Robert Venturi's *Complexity and Contradiction in Architecture*, shook the architectural world as violently as the dynamiting of the Pruitt-Igoe housing block in 1972, it embraced the notion that the space of the city in particular – the largest and most complex of all man-made artefacts, the one that is the most significant manifestation of our evolving civilizations – should not be the product of a totalitarian, unified geometric vision but should be conceived as a juxtaposition of highly differentiated spatial fragments.

This pluralist understanding of space is closer to our spontaneous experience of the richness of life and of the complexity of the environment around us, both in nature and in man-made spaces that have evolved historically.

By challenging the exclusive domination of Euclidean space, Postmodernism's more catholic interests opened the door to other geometries and morphogenetic processes: fractal, deconstructivist, organic, biomorphic, algorythmic, parametric... and included the important and radical notion that space is also entitled not to be organized consciously at all, that it may be allowed to be formed by chance, by accident – a proposition that contemporary design experiments are only just beginning to explore.

The resultant liberation of space from the straightjacket of Modernism is without doubt one of the most radical achievements of the Postmodernist period.

## Time

In the same way that it attempted to place itself outside contingent space and sought to replace it by ideal space, Modernism also endeavoured to place itself outside time, on the timeless *tabula rasa* of the avant-garde, cut off from the past.

Paradoxically, this uncompromising commitment to the 'here and now' leads to being neither here nor now: by ignoring the passage of time, by not acknowledging that we are living a chronological palimpsest of successive layers, time is deprived of its essence and of the necessary unpredictability of change. It stands to reason that the freshness of the present and the possibility of the future can only be experienced within the context of time.

The impoverishment of architectural and urban space resulting from Modernism's reluctance to preserve (or rather its desire to eradicate) the traces of previous historical spaces (as evidenced, for example, by Le Corbusier's Plan Voisin for Paris, which called for the complete destruction of medieval Paris) led also to a paralysis of time: it enveloped the modernist project within the frozen illusion of a suspended moment that appeared to want to last forever, to exercise its temporal monopoly over both past and future, and therefore became paradoxically retrospective, the unconsciously nostalgic 'rear-view mirror' effect of all architectural utopias.

Postmodernism re-addressed the issue of architecture's historical precedents. It attempted to put architecture back into the context of time. In doing so, it took it upon itself to explore design options that were hitherto considered to be forbidden territory, often transgressing the limits of 'good taste'. With projects happily plundering the vocabulary of neoclassicism and of the vernacular, it stood accused, and rightly so, of flattering reactionary appetites (of the aspiring petit bourgeois and residual aristocrat alike) by offering superficial and conventional codes of erudition, authority and make-believe respectability, all on the cheap. In many cases, these projects were indeed nothing but shallow pastiche, the products of commercial opportunism, especially when dealing with corporate office programmes.

But in the best of cases, we have to admit that they were playful, witty and irreverent expansions of the repertoire of architecture, extending its vocabulary to include elements that, thankfully, did not even claim to be 'authentic' – quite the contrary. It was a game of pastiche and illusion, flirting with the seduction of appearances, not claiming to be real, cultivating a trompe-l'oeil effect. The best examples were tongue-in-cheek hybrids, juxtaposing codes that were hacked, irreverently and inconsistently, from different periods in architectural history (including, ironically, Modernism) and creating eclectic hybrids that freely combined state-of-the-art engineering and contemporary materials with a profusion of references to ancient motifs. Terry Farrell's temporary 'Clifton Nurseries 2' project in Covent Garden is a wonderful example of such a hybrid.

All of the above were clearly the forbidden territories of Modernism, considered totally immoral by the orthodoxy.

The most positive outcome of this renewed interest in history, and in the rehabilitation of the values of heritage, was its impact on urbanism: it lead, in practice, to the increased adoption of preservation and regeneration schemes, mixing the old and the new, as opposed to the wholesale demolitions and redevelopments prevalent under the previous regime, which resulted in more lasting damage to our cities, worldwide, than the devastation inflicted by two successive world wars.

## Meaning

Just as Postmodernism opened up a different attitude to space, allowing designers, architects and urbanists to nurture its intrinsic complexity, and just as it allowed us again to appreciate the flow of time, it also questioned the draconian regime under which architecture had been put with respect to the meaning(s) it was permitted to convey.

Under Modernism, architecture was severely restricted in terms of what it was allowed to say. Predominantly, it was expected to be self-referential, not to seek to mean anything but a tautological expression of itself, to signify its own primary function and nothing else. The best option was to be essentially laconic. A building had to 'honestly' and directly reveal nothing but its purpose, its internal organization, its mode of fabrication, its structure, its materiality. It had to have no hidden secrets. Total transparency was the ideal model, and indeed dematerialized designs as well as the technology of glazing both evolved rapidly and simultaneously to meet this bizarre obsession for the truth alone.

No ambiguity was tolerated, no mixed messages, no contradictions, no paradoxes, no puns, no slips of the tongue, no riddles, no non-sense, no jokes, no lies, no attempts at seduction, no symbolic references, no allegories, no slang, no local dialects, no foreign inflections, no hesitations, no fragility, no contradictions, no changes of mind, no allusions, no excess, no generosity, no emotions, no dark desires, no touches of evil. An extraordinary set of injunctions of quasi-religious integrism that severely restricted the freedom, pleasure, depth and cultural relevance of architectural expression. It would be hard to imagine such a set of restrictions ever being imposed, for any length of time, on literature, music or the culture of cinema!

The Modernist paradigm was so restrictive in terms of its views on space, time and meaning that it had to impose strict rules of endoctrination to ensure that design remained within what it considered to be acceptable limits – rules of ascetism, purism, minimalism, virtuous restraints that threatened to cut down architecture to its simplest expression. These rules were self-imposed, unwritten rules at first but they eventually became codified by our professional bodies and reinforced by a building industry that benefited immensely from their simplicity and consistency, and the repetitive nature of the formula.

The fact that so many architects accepted, and for so long, to work within these ideological restrictions can only be explained by the fact that they were in the process of discovering a new language and that the fascination of this discovery, which had its own pleasures and clearly led to an extraordinary enrichment of the language of architecture, seemed to justify temporarily sacrificing a large part of its range of expression. Maybe the further evolution of architecture was only possible because of this immense sacrifice.

Of course individual architects with talent and an independent mind were able to play with these rules while appearing to remain within the fold of Modernism, so there were many early signs of Postmodernism long before the paradigm shift became manifest. Indeed this climate of austerity could not last. The architectural object could not be expected to forever express such a limited acception of 'the real' when, as Jean Baudrillard was to put it, 'reality is of such little importance' in an age of simulacra and simulations. Postmodernism took the lid off all these monastic restrictions. It made us understand that there was something pathological about Modernism's collective hallucination of sainthood, in its ascetic desire to say as little as possible, except for the obvious. The backlash was inevitable. At the end of the day, the repressed always comes to the surface and has the upper hand.

By allowing the architectural object to exercise its legitimate autonomy in relation to function and to take on meaning again, to embark upon all kinds of narratives, to embrace symbolism, to let buildings be allegories of something else, to convey feelings and emotions, to cultivate singularities, Postmodernism, in its all-embracing pluralism, imposed no restrictions: architecture was suddenly under no obligation to endorse any transcendent values nor to make any sense at all. It was free to have no meaning, to cultivate, if it so wished, the seduction of illusions, to become nothing but an illusion.

This opening up of the language also meant allowing the digital languages of the information age and 'virtual reality' to develop the new meanings that they are now able to generate, and, in particular, unpredictable meanings that are not imposed deterministically, that are not under our design control.

## Legacy

So where do we stand now? What has been achieved?

The biggest achievement, in conceptual and philosophical terms, is that Postmodernism has given us, not just in architecture but in the other arts as well, a far more diverse set of variables with which to apprehend the world; to borrow from the terminology of cybernetics and information theory, we are now better equipped to fulfil the 'law of requisite variety', which states that any knowledge tools we use in order to understand a system (and intervene within it) must have at least the same 'quantity of variety' as the system under scrutiny.

This increase in the degree of 'variety' of our knowledge has made it possible for us to fully acknowledge the multidimensional and multi-scalar complexity of design, from that of interiors (which this book is ostensibly about) to cities.

It is, in my opinion, our understanding of cities that has benefited the most, precisely because it is our most diverse and complex artefact, and therefore the one that suffers most from generalizations and oversimplifications. The work of Terry Farrell in this respect is exemplary. In his many writings about the city, and London in particular, and also through his international practice, he has drawn our attention to the specificity of context and to the richness of historical evolution. He has found inventive ways of resolving what Colin Rowe called 'the crisis of the object', the tendency that Modernist architects had of treating buildings as isolated objects (as exemplified, famously, by Le Corbusier's project for Saint-Die) rather than as part of a continuous urban tissue. Terry Farrell, in a characteristically pluralist way, has managed in his work to solve Rowe's impossible riddle and satisfy both aspirations: to give the context pride of place and to give the object a chance to shine.

Our increased awareness of the complexity, variety and availability of information in post-industrial society raises the issue of authorship, and one of the key legacies of postmodernism has been the shift from the culture of the single author to that of multiple hands. This has become particularly apparent and topical in the multidisciplinary, collective work currently undertaken on the city and the public realm.

Some say that Postmodernism is over, but that is not logically possible. Once an advanced civilization, under the impulse of a major change in its modes of production, knowledge and communication, has gone through such a comprehensive process of emancipation and decolonization – affecting not just its architecture and urbanism, but all its cultural mores – it cannot go back in time.

The world of so-called late capitalism has definitely become more pluralistic, politically as well as culturally: in our age of ubiquitous access to communications media, the big meta-narratives have lost their resonance and their grip.

In retrospect, one sometimes wonders if they have ever had such a powerful hold on us. Was Modernism really so absolutist and unpliable in its ideology, so relentlessly monolithic? Did it not allow, after all, a brilliantly diverse series of 'small narratives' to come into existence? Was the critical reaction at times exaggerated? And, conversely, did Postmodernism not seek also to impose its own conceits, its own conventions?

Now that the heroic epoch of neoclassical pastiche is largely over, fortunately, we realize that such stylistic architectural provocations are not what Postmodernism has been about. What is significant is that the cultural engagement and vocabulary of architecture have been significantly expanded in numerous ways. It is irrelevant to ask whether Postmodernism has finally absorbed Modernism or if it is the other way round; the enrichment of our vocabulary is clearly the result of the combined effect and interlocking of both movements and it does not really matter how you put it.

The distinct ideologies behind both movements are still alive and the growing threat of globalization is now far more dangerous than the conditions were last century when the polemic started, when hedgehogs and foxes had their little skirmishes. Now that the stakes are so much higher, the late confrontations between Modernists and Postmodernists, virulent as they may have seemed at times, will be perceived as child's play.

# 1

# Home Interiors

Terry Farrell

This book centres on the view of architecture and city planning as a continuous flow of scales in which the city may essentially be viewed as a large house, and the house as a small city. The home, the subject of this chapter, is at the smallest end of that scale continuum, but nevertheless it has to be able to serve as a container for a community of many different people, with different needs and different ways of living and expressing themselves.

Le Corbusier famously described the house as 'a machine for living in': a designed product that is complete within itself, that works with every part contributing, with no redundancy, stripped back to its essential rule of efficiency and order; like the car engine or the car itself. It is a product of industrial design, ergonomics and so on. Throughout the world today, though – and particularly in the UK – the vast majority of people live in buildings that were not conceived for i.e. not 'designed for' twenty-first-century lifestyles. With levels of construction activity in the UK and much of the West unlikely ever to reach the height they did in the nineteenth and twentieth centuries, the legacy of the earlier building booms provides as good a starting point as any for the creation of homes in our cities, towns and villages. The surplus of hospitals, factories, grand single and terraced houses and apartment blocks can be treated as 'found objects' and adapted to suit modern needs. As we will see in this chapter, the Postmodern view of 'home' that evolved during the 1970s and 80s is quite different to the 'machine for living in', to the Modernist designed 'object'.

The four houses shown here began life, as one would expect, in quite different ways. Our house in Ashworth Road, Maida Vale was built in 1924, in the aftermath of World War I, when cottage-style houses were springing up across large swathes of north-west London. Servant-less, compact, and manageable by a family on its own, these homes continued elements of the Garden City movement which had begun some two decades before. Their three-up, two-down format is still a model for much of the mass housing in the United Kingdom. When set in the middle of a complex city rather than among green fields, they have an interface with historical urban layering that differentiates them from their Garden City predecessors. Tube lines run underneath them, excavations have changed the height of the ground, and so on. When we purchased our house in 1974, it was virtually unaltered, having had only one previous owner who had bought it new.

The factory at Hatton Street in Marylebone, on the other hand, had gone through several different occupants – from a building component manufacturer (first building 1919) mainly based on timber, to an aircraft factory (1940), followed by several years of vacancy (1982–85, immediately before I arrived) and it has been through several iterations since, whilst I have been in occupation there. At first, it was an office for our architectural practice, then it became a private studio for me, and latterly it has been my permanent home with my new wife. In the days of the architectural practice the basement area that is now our private studio was the storage workshop; prior to that it had been the boiler room. So it has supported many different uses. We occupy two separate parts, in effect parts of six floors of the building, but there are 16 other flats, maisonettes and studios in the rest of it. The accident of the distribution of rooms, their size and form, the staircases, the spaces – it was all part of some predecessor's designed and planned idea of where everything should be, reflecting its original uses and ownerships. Just like the Ashworth Road house, it was based on what was seen as the most desirable special combination for the market at the time it was built. But of course, the same needs do not apply today: the factory becomes studios that become homes. Clearly not a case of 'form following function'.

Adaptations, I believe, provide some of the most fascinating spaces. For example the Architectural Association (AA), one of the most respected architectural institutions in the world, occupies a row of buildings in London's Bedford Square that were intended for an entirely different use to the one it has now. It is a group of differently planned eighteenth-century family houses that have been adapted to become a school of architecture. The tall, thin houses were homes belonging to a different age, catering to the privileged families of the time, with servants' quarters, grand dining rooms, coal-fired heating and virtually no plumbing. I find the interface between the original design purpose and today's use, as well as the layers of what happened in between, extremely stimulating architecturally. It's all part of using chance, using chaos to bring a new kind of dynamic order, an order of being settled at any point in time, differently to an earlier point in time. It is almost as if one is living in a garden of human life and of human interactions within an inanimate world of floors, roofs, staircases – made of concrete, steel and glass in the case of the factory, or bricks and tiles in the case of the house. There's a kind of organic stewardship that reminds me very much of Darwin's 'tangled bank', but here it's the human life that lives within our cities, within our homes. If the city is a large house then it is a very large tangled bank indeed, and a house a very small one. Not only did Darwin feel there was grandeur in all of this, but he also saw there was order: an order that was not based on pre-design, but one in which adaptive design were continuous and mutating. In the same way our homes, our microcosms of house and city, undertake this organic, naturally evolving self-ordering process.

One of the dramatic characteristics, one might say, of a Postmodern era is the tolerance of different tastes, and the idea that homes, interiors, cities are the product not only of a historical variance over time, but also of personality types and taste types – so that children, husbands, wives, partners can make contributions, their presence can be expressed. A home must evolve with the people inside it, according to their needs and life experiences. Some of the interiors in this chapter, particularly at Ashworth Road and Hatton Street, are shown here at different stages, to illustrate the changes in financial circumstances, aspirations, and to some extent taste. The home at Ashworth Road owes a lot to my then wife Sue Farrell, who designed tiling and carpets and did so much of the organizing of the final occupation in terms of furniture and ambience and character, the things we were surrounded with and the things we could touch. There is the very essence of interactive responsiveness to context, to the house itself, its walls and its occupation by the family community.

Our excitement and enthusiasm about the context of our homes can be expressed in our response to 'as found' interiors. The interior of the factory studio at Hatton Street is very much a response to the metal, the steel roof trusses, the concrete floor, the stripped windows, the big industrial roof lights – and also to its external context, to the kind of rawness of the surrounding streets, which are still a working area even though the factory's labour force is long gone. It is statistically one of the most deprived wards in the whole of London, yet it is

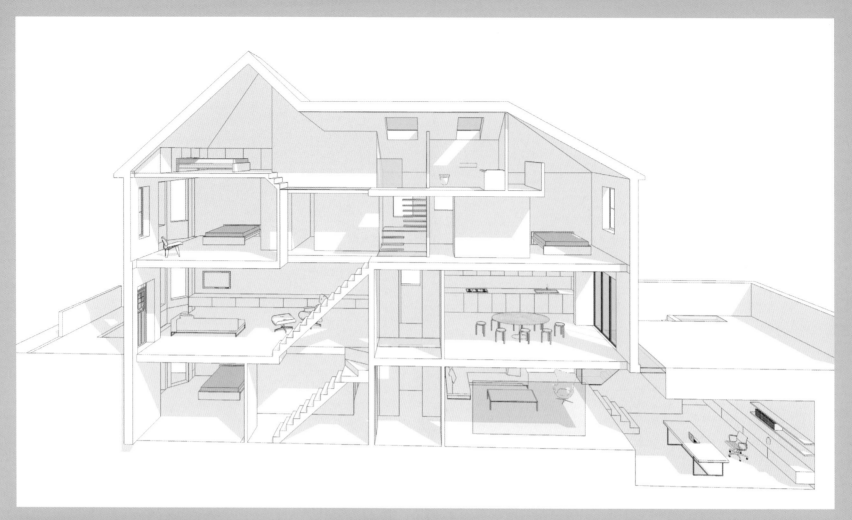

Above: Section of the contemporary home of George Clarke – an architect who once worked in the TFP office. Although the architectural expression is different, so many of the spatial strategies parallel those in Farrell's own house in Maida Vale – and indeed many other homes in London. For younger generations exploring spatial complexity and richness within the shell of a house from earlier times is now architecturally as challenging and valid as building new.

Left: The house of Farrell's client and friend John Scott (he is an antique collector). Farrell helped him with parts of the house at its early stages; over the years it has become a maximalist's tour-de-force.

adjacent to prosperous St John's Wood, Maida Vale and Bayswater. The local street market sells bric-a-brac and odds and ends, and bringing all these artefacts back into the house connects them and me to the neighbourhood. What I bought from market stalls, from the antiques shops and from other odd shops along Church Street over the years – things that took my fancy, things that looked amusing, things that I can't imagine finding anywhere but there – added to and enriched the interior of the home over several decades.

This sense of the context of place, of identification with the city around a building, is part and parcel of the Postmodern notion of buildings as place-makers. 'Ideal' cities commissioned from scratch – Brasília, Chandigarh, Milton Keynes – take time to develop the layered quality that makes them human. London's liveableness has a lot to do with its successful integration of the said layering, with the interrelationship balancing between old and new.

At our house on Ashworth Road we have a well established, mature context, with the street's rear gardens laid out so that the original purchasers in the 1920s could each claim to have their own little bit of territory to plant vegetables or trees or lawn. These have all congealed together into one bio-sustainable unit. There have been fascinating recent studies which show that species that have been dying out in the countryside as a result of industrialised farming, are now flourishing in the back gardens of many of the city residential neighbourhoods of London which are recognised as potentially possessing more ecological richness than parts of the very countryside itself. Almost every family home outside the central core of the city has a front garden and a back garden with low separating walls. Looking across them can often be like looking across a piece of woodland countryside in town. It has been said that the total area of private gardens in central London is greater than all of the royal and public parks put together. Indeed because of their variety, and because of the separate ownership and the density in which they occur, there is a richness of life here that you just don't get in the parks, which tend to be more designed, managed and manicured. In our backyard in Maida Vale I've seen more foxes, frogs, hedgehogs, herons, jays, owls, and birds I'd never recognise than I ever have in the country or urban park. Coupled with the rich plant life that the Englishman puts in his garden – some quite exotic, some self-seeding – you have one of the finest garden landscape features of any city, anywhere. And one can experience it all just by opening the back door.

I referred earlier to the effect of allowing chance into modern design endeavours, in a Postmodern view of the world. The false order of a 'perfect' interior such as Mies van der Rohe's Farnsworth House in Plano, Illinois (1951) has no place in ordinary daily life. The Farnsworth House was after all a seldom-occupied, second-home folly, only in use for a few months of the year. When I saw it on touring America in the 1960s, it was totally boarded up and seemed abandoned. It is not a home; it's a demonstration of an architectural idea, it's almost a piece of designer branding, it's a marketing exercise, a vehicle for a particular set of rather abstract architectural ideas. It may well be a sublime essay in abstraction, based loosely on the idea of a 'house', but it is certainly not a home. The home has to have the element of chance and time and ordered chaos. It has to have a spatial discontinuity, and the complexity of decorative and personal expression. The minimalist idea of creating order in chaos is a kind of aristocratic elitist order wherein a house or apartment is walled off from the disorder of the uncontrollable, real-life chaos outside its boundaries. But one day the walls will be breached – one day the order, the appearance of order will inevitably go, history has always shown us that. Leaders in industry and commerce, whose livelihoods depend on risk-taking, on excitement, on being on the edge of chaos, often revert to minimalism in the design of their homes. Their houses may be minimalist and pure, but newspapers constantly tell us that their lives are far more complex, exotic and extraordinary than any of us more ordinary people can ever imagine. This minimalism is a kind of false order, a reassurance of power and separateness and give an illusion of being in control. At a more alarming level, we hear that Le Corbusier made approaches to the Nazis to see if they would be interested in his plans for demolishing central Paris and rebuilding it according to his vision. The Nazis, in their despotic, ruthless centralism, would surely have been delighted to impose such a so-called order upon any city. Thankfully, of course, better judgements prevailed. Paris in all its complexity and layering has far more value to it than any designed city despotically created top-down at one point in time.

Spatial complexity is a particularly interesting aspect of the home. All architect friends of mine have indulged a desire for exploring just how rich a space within a house can become. Stephen Marshall – one of my former students and employees, and indeed a tenant in my own house in Maida Vale at one time – has designed an extraordinarily complex

house in Camden Town. So has George Clarke, another ex-employee now with his own practice, who has made so many spatial changes to his home it really parallels our Maida Vale house but in another era with different architectural tastes. He has dug down into the back garden, extended the basement, capitalised on roof spaces to form a void above the top-floor ceiling, and created vision lines and light wells to connect the floors one to another. It is an essay in complexity and spatial excitement that reflects all the different occupants and their different skills and sensibilities – that little children for example, love to creep under things, how they see the space under the table as a complete home, a house within a house. So the home becomes a kind of set of Russian dolls. The adaptable spaces cater for everything from a large party to a small dinner gathering, from the nuclear family right down to just a child on its own.

Working through the requirements of these different sets of scales and occupants is a critical part of the interpretation of home by architects and designers of London homes. Loft and basement spaces become ever more essential and indeed the very positioning of these various spatial types reinforces differences, reinforces place. Postmodernist space and place were always emphasising what is highly particularised rather than what is universal and repetitive. The 'roof-ness' of modern homes – whether it's six floors up in our factory loft or just the inhabited loft space of a small semi-detached or terraced house – brings with it triangulation of shape and exposure to structure, but also immediately enhances all our senses and awareness of the bigger environment – aeroplanes flying overhead, a fire engine or police siren in the distance, and in particular the quiet of the morning. One hears the birds more; passing seagulls and nesting blackbirds sit on the roof, and the dawn chorus is really appreciated. And of course there are also different views from up here, giving a new rooftop perspective of the city.

At the bottom, the basement is a world of quietness, of walls and solidity. It's where many more pictures can be hung, where you can store things without having to worry about fluctuations in temperature, and where in many houses – such as ours in Maida Vale – late at night you can hear the very quiet distant rumble of the Tube trains passing by, maybe 100 feet below.

Then of course there is what is one of the great triumphs of the English house type: the ground floor. Ground is the great floorplan of cities. In spite of the efforts in the 1950s and 60s to introduce raised pedestrian access areas around cities and urban redevelopment complexes, the cities and urban redevelopment complexes, the ground plane remains pre-eminent. Apart from anything else, you can plant things in it and they grow. But also there is none of the friction that is caused by a change of level: you can enter and leave front and back fairly spontaneously, so that the garden becomes an extension of the interior, a place for gazebos and conservatories and sheds or just simply lawns to sit on. Many adaptations of Victorian and twentieth-century traditional houses in London have involved opening up walls and inserting sliding glazed doors borrowed from Modernism – from the roof terrace of Le Corbusier's Villa Savoye near Paris (1928–31), or from the West Coast houses of Canada's Arthur Erickson, bits are collaged into the existing home. You do not have to live in a Modernist icon in order to enjoy that illusion of spatial transition; it has been replicated in the back walls of brick terraces and semi-detached houses all over London's inner and outer areas.

In the end it's all about extending and adding and giving value to the home and, through it, to the family living in it. As the homes illustrated here demonstrate, when colour and expression are injected into the structure of a house, it can become a delight for the whole family – right down to making it a place that children want their friends to visit and stay in. It's a kind of stewardship but it is also an expression of joy and occupation.

For so many in Britain, homeownership is a critical part of expression. It is something the average person can have in common with the most established and wealthy of aristocrats: just as the Duke of Westminster could own the Mayfair estate, so you can own your own little bit of an 'estate' within, a bit of suburbia or inner central London. You can have somewhere to invest your efforts over time, somewhere to nurture, because everything you do to it will not only enrich your own life but also add to the financial value of the house, in terms of making it more appealing to a potential future buyer. My house in Maida Vale, which I owned for 30 years, appreciated year on year in value more than I was earning by going out every day to work in an architect's office, and this had a significant effect on my practising as an architect. I started off with no money, coming from a family of working people in the north of England, and whenever there was a threat of economic recession, with a consequent impact upon the construction industry, I was able to borrow against the house and pay the office rent and wages. In that way its value fuelled the very business that I was carrying forward – it was like the Duke's Mayfair, my cherished primary asset that made the world work for me.

I now come to the fourth of the houses that I have chosen for inclusion in this chapter – the Thematic House (1979–84), a collaboration principally between me, the architectural writer and landscape architect Charles Jencks and his wife Maggie. I think it important to separate the Jencks house from the other three because it has many characteristics that are not common to the others – not least the very conscious and deliberate collaborative process of which it was a product. It was much more a home that was designed for the record, for architectural posterity. Its creation involved many other well-known figures: Piers Gough designed a Jacuzzi, Eduardo Paolozzi combined components of staircases and inlaid artistic features, Michael Graves designed fireplaces, and so on. The project lasted for nearly five years, and many of the architects working on it in our office at the time went on to found practices of their own, but at the time it was seen as a real opportunity to work with myself and the Jencks' and to explore what became a built exemplar of Postmodernist expression. It began as an adaptation of a 'found object', an end-of-terrace Victorian house – the kind that Stefan Muthesius wrote about in his great book *The English Terraced House* (1982). Once the big decisions about the concept of the spaces had been made, and the restructuring and rebuilding had happened, Charles began a programme of personal occupied expression to turn the house into a defining statement of his position on Postmodernism. It was and is, in this respect, a demonstration project, just as Mies van der Rohe's Barcelona Pavilion (1929) was of Modernism in its time. The post-rationalised symbolism of the decorative layer which Charles imposed upon the house has made the photographing of the building today irrevocably slanted towards his own vision as the veneer, the decorative overlay is the very surface, the immediate imagery you see first. It was Charles' intention that the style and manner, the dress, the fashion of Postmodernism would be on show here, and in that sense it was quite separate from my own perception of what Postmodernism, or even a home, is all about.

In a sense the Thematic House was two projects in one. Firstly, there was the project structure's architecture, the organisation of the spaces and the general architectural direction which included the concept of seasons revolving around the central stair 'the sun'. It then drilled down to the architectural structure of how the trusses worked, how this translated into expression – for example, the precast staircase treads were part of the symbolism of days, weeks and years. All of this we led on. But the second project was led by Charles, and I suppose in a sense it was cathartic for me and many who worked on it. For Charles it was the expression of Postmodernism – of its visual and stylistic characteristics, and of the symbolic rationale behind it. Over the course of the project, we learnt the limits of Postmodernism as a style, when it was not and could not be a style at all. And with today's hindsight, it was somewhat contradictory to search for a defining visual style; Postmodernism was an antidote to the era of metanarratives, it was a liberating era and the only failure was that some wanted to give it an overall visual control again – replacing emperor with another emperor, as it were. For me the TV-am headquarters (1981–3), Embankment Place (1987–90) and many of the things I did at the time were much more eclectic, much more complex visually working at many levels. The best architects that emerged from this shift, this era of Postmodernism became more and more liberated and more independent of an overall conforming style – theirs was a free-spirited and liberated architectural expression, such as Stirling, Alsop, Gehry, Nouvel, Isozaki. All attempts at 'inventing' a visual style for Postmodernism seemed like thin, unconvincing overlays. Many who had their feet firmly in the previous era, stuck in the 1970s, judged this new era in its own terms. They looked for an overall unifying 'consistent' visual expression and often quite rightly recoiled at any attempts they saw that tried to supply an overall apparent answer that replaced their view. But there were no singular answers any more, and any attempts to provide one contradicted the very spirit of the Postmodern times we were, and still are, in.

The house was quite a point of departure for me, particularly when it was used extensively as an exposition of Charles' views in the many books and magazines that demonstrated his Postmodern thinking. Charles' view of the house, we often commented, was inevitably driven by its potential to position his architectural theories. Working on it probably deterred me from continuing with Postmodernism as a singular architectural expression. It led me to be much more interested in narrative and collage, and in particular city planning and urban design, becoming involved in projects like Mansion House and the Hammersmith roundabout through the 1980s, dealing with urban planning issues, particularly on behalf of lobby and community groups or conservation agencies like Save and English Heritage. But visual language aside, the Thematic House (Jencks' title) is a really worthwhile exploration and indeed a considerable achievement in terms of spatial complexity, of adaptation, of collaboration – all the things I have come to love and work with during my career.

The legacy of the Postmodern home lies in the way it moved everything on. All three of the building types discussed in this book – the museum, the workplace, and in particular the home – are complex, many-tiered, many-layered. The concept of there being a pre-ordained, pre-designed machine for collective living in may work for a small group of middle-class people in one situation in France, as at Ronchamp, but it is not relevant for most of the world's population. Le Corbusier's urban ideas as a foundation for good city making and mass social housing in particular was shattered by the destruction first of Ronan Point in London and then Pruit Igoe in the US. What became obvious was that there were far more significant issues for the architect–planner to get involved in than merely the design of the ideal or standardised 'designed' house: the outside, the urbanism of the housing estates, the notion of 'home' and of a collection of homes – all these were clearly of much greater importance for the architect and planner. The designed mechanics of the home, the walls and the enclosures or rather the engineering of the walls and the enclosures were not the big issue; in fact they could be readily done in many different way. Even though architects often justified these projects through the need to provide mass housing quickly, the answer was not necessarily to be found in prefabrication. Indeed it was generally proven that with bricks laid one on top of the other you could build houses pretty quickly, and in fact for the most part as quickly as people needed them in most European countries.

So in housing technology and innovation is not the issue. What is the issue is planning layout, of streets and neighbourhoods, was housing management, including maintenance, was rental strategies and the very suitability of housing types for the people who would be dwelling in them. Choice – not top-down dictate – became increasingly the issue. Do working people really want to be in tower blocks? Do they really want to have their terraced houses demolished? And do they want all their communities broken up to move to estates – however wonderful the bathrooms and kitchens and plumbing might be there? Along with that went the question of stewardship: do people really want to move to a place where everything is reliant on a centralised system, with the accompanying requirement of maintenance of lifts and district heating systems? Do they really want to walk out into a vast realm of common land rather than their own back garden? And do they really want to leave behind their own individual front door in favour of one leading into 100 flats or so, where they need a concierge to enforce security? (But one had never been offered.) Without investment in custodianship and stewardship, these new (modern) forms of housing provision disintegrated socially, with a rise in crime and the abandonment of flats – the decay and collapse depicted in J G Ballard's novel *High Rise* (1975) became a reality for many of the Western world's social housing estates.

But in time, with a totally different kind of occupancy and stewardship, the 'sink estates' could be brought back into use. Many of them already have been; after all, as they are a resource to be recycled, to be adapted and evolve new uses. The Trellick Tower (Ernö Goldfinger, 1966–72) is now sought after by yuppies, who approach the building in a different way – making their mark on it, making themselves at home. The recognition of the hand of the occupant is crucial, as are security and the management of outdoor spaces. There's many a happy, successful housing scheme that you would pass by without noticing – and we have designed some of them ourselves. These haven't won awards because the architects weren't trying to get them, they were just creating homes for people: terraced houses, small suburban infills, conversions of existing houses and factories into flats, and great stately homes subdivided. In all of this, architectural expression and experimentation was not particularly high on the agenda.

So Postmodernist thinking has changed our perception of how to create homes for today. When an architect's focus is too much on the external visual statement made by a building, the occupants' potential for self-expression tends to get forgotten, as does the interrelationship between the home and its urban environment. That is not to say that a building with a strong sense of architectural style cannot work well, of course; but for most buildings, other things come first. We have moved from the Modernist concept of the designed object to a looser notion of a place that must be adaptable, allowing a series of occupants to make their mark on it and over time. Home is a place for living in, breathing, growing, changing, and for all the people in it, and for all the people in the street and in the neighbourhood and the city around.

# Family Home, Maida Vale

The house in which Terry Farrell lived for 15 years placed him very much in the planning of London in the 1910s to 20s. It is located in Ashworth Road, a single street of semi-detached 20s houses that were built in a different era from the rest of Maida Vale – suburban semis.

Ashworth Road has its own character, as so much of London does. The road is not just suburban; it is a collage, a layer. It is so obviously one of London's many accidents of timing – a kind of drama in slow motion of a city shaping and forming itself.

Maida Vale, one of the main arteries that leads traffic out of London to the North, is a result of the Bakerloo Line following the old Roman road of Watling Street to Edgware and beyond, creating new residential areas. Ashworth Road was delayed in its construction because excavated soil produced by work on the Bakerloo Line between Warwick Avenue and Maida Vale was dumped here, which meant that between 1910 and the mid-1920s the road was just fields. The soil was taken up a vertical shaft and spread over the area. As a result, the fields were a metre higher than the surrounding area. The soil itself, though, had been 20 metres below the ground, which meant that the very ground itself was an added layer of urbanization with its own history.

The notion of space layered onto existing space was reflected in the Ashworth Road house; adapting and adding layers to an existing building created spatial character so that every room was unique. One went in the door to the circulation hall, went into a room that was four walls with a window and a fireplace on one side. But the space was transformed so that each floor had a uniqueness of character which came from a reinterpretation of the space that was there. The ground floor was all opened up so that the front and back rooms were joined and, since the floorboards had been taken out to link this area with the cellar, there was a spiral space that went from the lowest to the halfway level and then to the dining area, and eventually to a conservatory (added in the late 80s) and out to the garden. There was a spatial dynamic that came from the existing building; exploiting space and difference because of embedded character and exploiting that character was all part of Ashworth Road. There was also the quantity of space and the character of that space. And there was the inherent flexibility achieved by opening walls, by connecting horizontally.

Modernism is about consistency and universality. The outside reflects what is inside. By contrast Ashworth Road was layers of many styles, which challenged the Modernist ideal. The house was purposefully inconsistent – when one opened the door it revealed a treasure chest, which is why it became known as 'The Tardis'.

The home was a relaxed, free-spirited and undemanding canvas. It was not a statement about, it was not a business card, it was not an advert – but that in itself was the architectural style Farrell was evolving, where a pluralistic world based upon layering and the involvement of a range of people's emotions plus all their innate creativity as well as his, could be brought together. And so the house was a very significant piece. Rather than deliberately designing and drawing up this piece of work, as architects do, Farrell just let it happen around him and it fed back into his work.

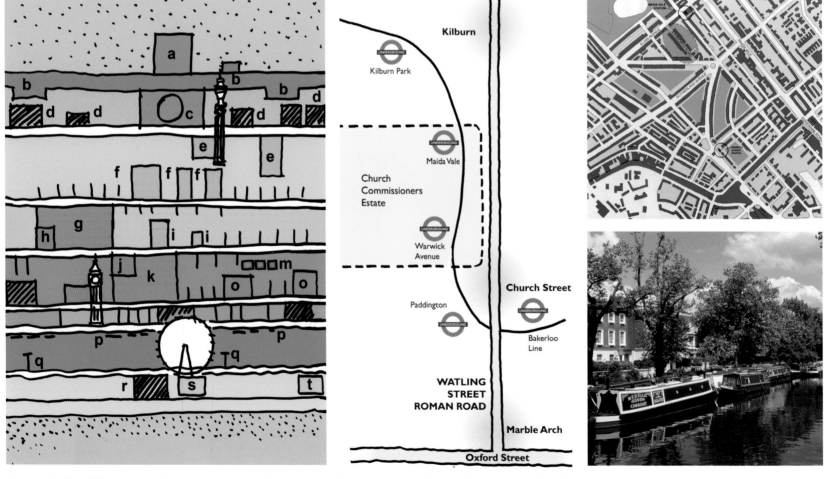

Bottom left: Farrell diagram showing London layers: social strata created by the main roads that graduate outwards from the Thames.

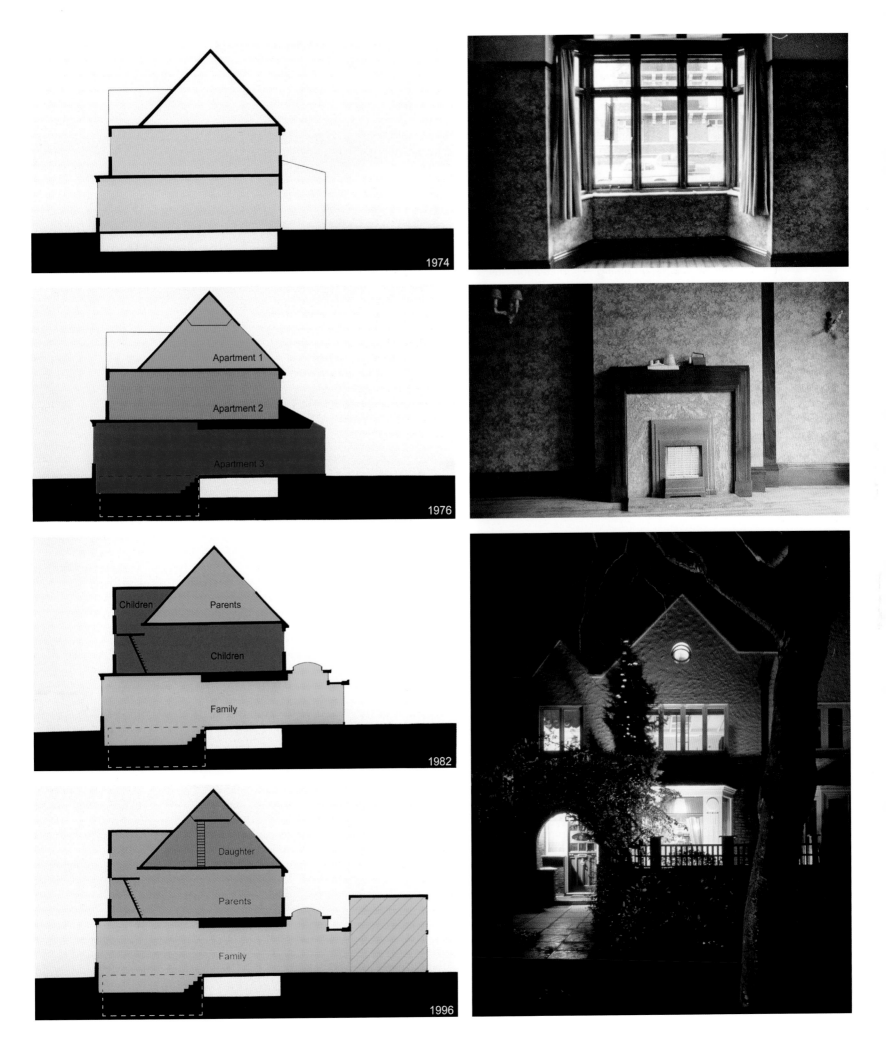

1974

1976

1982

1996

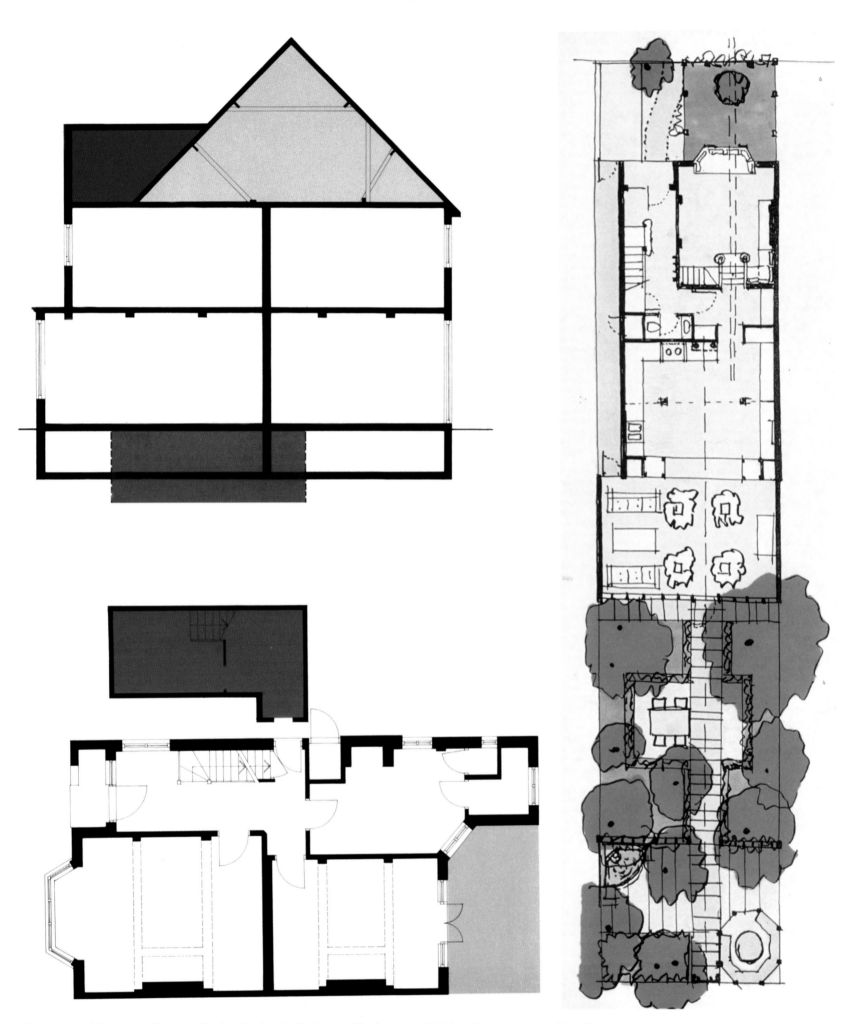

This page: (top) Section and (bottom left) plan showing the final stage of the house and (right) gardens and the principles of the internal space re-utilization.

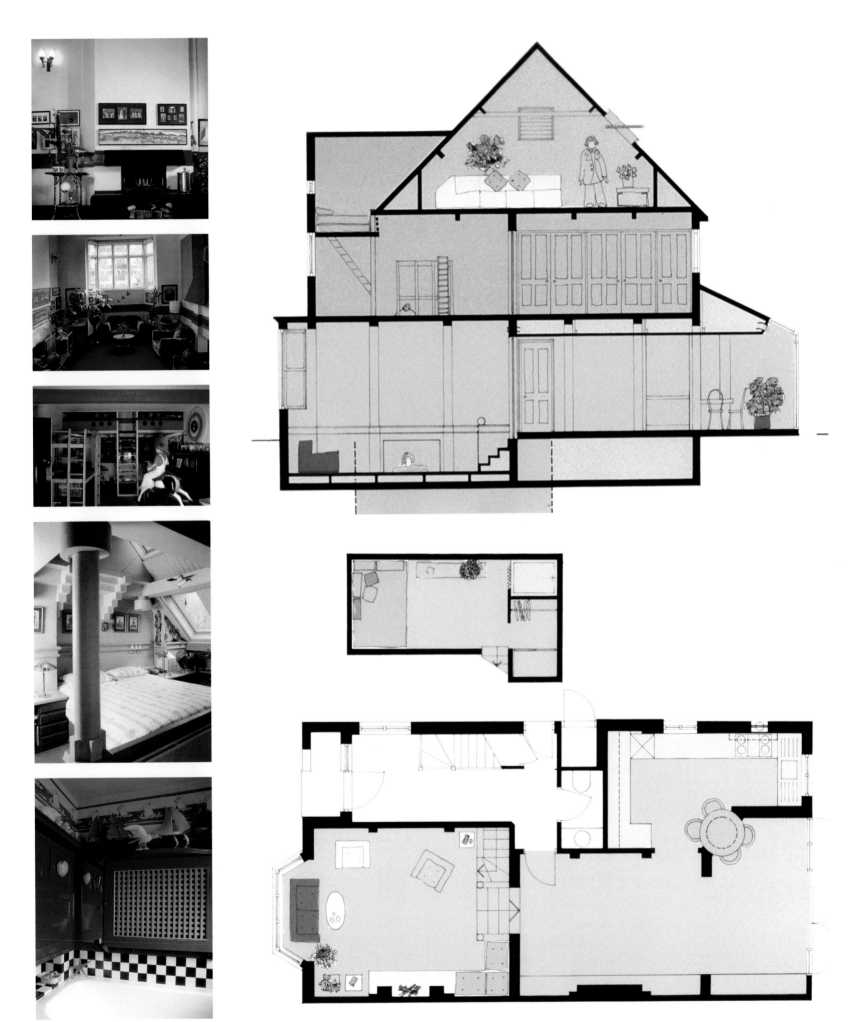

This page right: Plans and sections, intermediary stage early 1980s.

This page and opposite: The living areas with sunken living room. This page bottom right: Sculpture by Sokari Douglas Camp.

Opposite and top: The sunken living room. Bottom: Dining and kitchen areas, intermediary stage early 1980s.

This page and opposite: The main dining and kitchen area with tiling and carpet designed by Sue Farrell.

This page top: Kitchen area. Bottom and opposite: Entrance hallway and stair, with original varnishing and Anaglypta wallpaper retained from 1924.

This page and opposite: Conservatory, garden, and pavilion by Francis Machin.

# Family Home, Kensington

The Jencks House is in itself a built manifesto of Postmodernism.

The Jenckses had found that although they had their own architectural ideas, they were nevertheless unable to build the house they wanted. They needed an architect, and one who could be involved as a designer, so they approached Terry Farrell specifically. In 1978, Charles Jencks and Farrell jointly started the design process, with countless conceptual sketches and design and working drawings that explain in detail the evolution of the house.

The addition of a two-storey annexe, paired interlocking conservatories, a central spiral staircase and mirrored light shaft, among other features, created a dynamic space within which Jencks applied a symbolic programme based on the cosmos, the solar system and the seasons. The building was not preconceived symbolically in every detail; it evolved over many years and was as much a question of discovering latent symbolism as of imposing an *a priori* programme.

The Jenckses started with two basic ideas. The first was that the front of the building should be related to its context in the street. The second was spatial – using double-height spaces, an arcade to the garden and a sequence of stairs and terraces. Light, space and views were the obvious goals – a continuous space which would extend the eye and the imagination and that would be controlled by rooms which would essentially be closed and classical in form. Axes, cross-axes and simple geometrical forms would exist in plan, interrupted only at minor points. The result was a semi-open plan with fragmented classical shapes and an important diagonal axis connecting the two London columns (a diagonal which makes this space unusual for a London terraced house).

Charles Jencks had always wanted a theme for the house. At first, a lot of the theme work was based on the names and characters of his family. At a later stage, the house became the 'Terraced House' because of its three main terrace connections and its place within the tradition of the London terraced house. However, the final and basic theme for the house was the seasons. Even before this point the central staircase had been referred to as the 'Sun', both because of its passive solar heating potential and because it sat centrally within the house plan. It was Farrell's suggestion that, because of their orientation, the four zones of the house on the ground floor could each be allocated one of the four seasons around the Sun. Just as with the spatial formation and plan structure, the eventual symbolism was founded upon the very connections made within the essentially architectural process of developing a plan for a house.

Adding on to London terraced housing in order to extend the spatial volume of a house or to add modern amenities was the basis of many early projects at Farrells. Previous generations had a different attitude to the fronts and backs of houses: they did not value views over gardens or southern orientation, or the reduction of noise intrusion from the street. House plans were therefore standardized and not varied according to orientation or view.

The Postmodern space is highly particular. It is not a space in which the occupant is free to express whatever he likes; each part is allocated its role, then its character is set and its opportunities are explored by the designer rather than the occupant. The Jencks House constitutes a series of set pieces, which were resolved to a certain point of concept and detail. Layered onto these, then, is the personal decorative work of the owners, which has its own identity and story to tell.

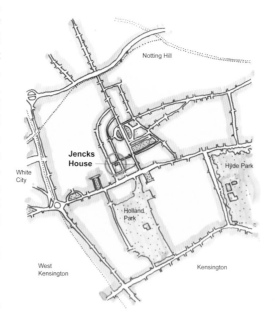

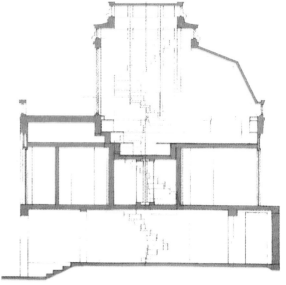

Top right: Section shows annexe roof. Bottom: Photographs of front and back of existing building prior to construction.

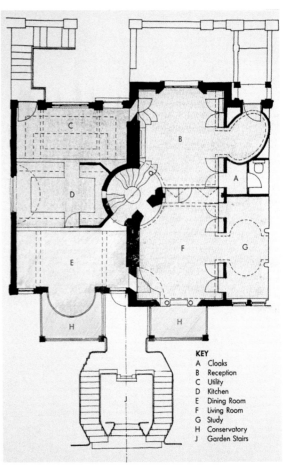

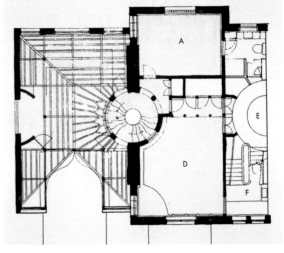
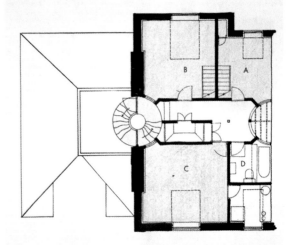

KEY
A  Cloaks
B  Reception
C  Utility
D  Kitchen
E  Dining Room
F  Living Room
G  Study
H  Conservatory
J  Garden Stairs

Top left: Seated area looking on to rear garden. Top middle: Child's bedroom. Bottom left: Stairwell face.

This page: Dining room.

This page right: Farrell office's study models.

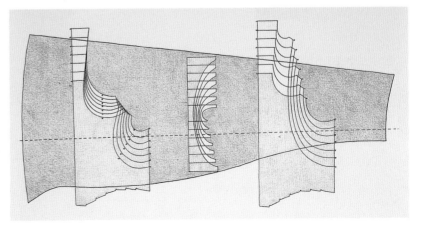

Bottom right: Detail drawing of staircase tread; these were 52 treads one for each week of the year; each was cast with seven elements.

Above left: The moonwell created by top light and mirrors.  Bottom right and opposite: The main staircase with Paolozzi mosaic.

# Family Home, Cambridgeshire

Upwood House was built during the Civil War; it belongs to the Caroline Period. The site is first mentioned first in the Chronicles of Ramsey Abbey as the home of Earl Ailwine, to whom it had been given by King Edgar. Despite its age, however, it is not an exceptional example of great architecture, due to the many changes that have been made to the house over the centuries.

When Ailwine died, the house passed to Sir Richard Williams, alias Cromwell, until 1648. At this point, the house was a large country farmhouse. In 1648, Judge Stephen Pheasant bought the Manor of Upwood and began building the larger house. In 1811 Richard Bickerton, second-in-command under Nelson, took over and added the Regency wing, which gave the house much wider reception rooms. The gardens were landscaped at this time too. In 1965, after the estate had been sold in lots, the house was bought by John and Jenny Moxon, who undertook further alterations and repairs.

In 1972 the property was sold to the architect Hilton Wright. Planning permission was granted to divide the house into two, and subsequently three, entirely different houses. The division occurred along existing walls. The north end of the house, called Ailwyn House, had its own entrance and drive. The south end, which retained the name Upwood House, received few structural changes: a partition dividing the old library at the back of the room, a study at the front and a simple staircase to the top floor. After these alterations it was sold to two families who converted the house even further. The wing added by Bickerton was one house – Farrell's family house – and the remaining part another. The barn and the stables, sold in 1975, were also converted into two further private houses.

The 1811 house looked entirely to the garden. It was basically a box, 6 x 9 metres. Originally, the ground floor was covered by a 10 x 10 grid; there was a fireplace next to a door towards the old house and five windows on the façade looking onto the garden. Upstairs was a small corridor and two big rooms. And that is all it was.

Addressing this grid, and attempting once again to gain extra space, the first transformation was to make one of the five windows – the middle one – a front door. This window, in the centre of the south elevation, was extended to the ground, forming an opening so that little external change was apparent. It was created almost as an invisible door, leaving the rhythm of the façade unbroken.

On the ground floor, the stairs were positioned in the northeast corner of the old ballroom. This is now a platform room that extends out from where the double doors into the drawing room used to be. The balcony was positioned there in order to have the least amount of staircase; a window was opened in the ceiling and four columns were positions to make the platform possible. The columns hold up not only the mezzanine but also the new walls of the floor above.

The first floor, following the existing grid, was divided into four bedrooms, two on each side of the lobby; the bathroom was in the middle and a cloakroom and a cupboard next to it. The staircase continued up as a hidden staircase behind the cupboard. The ceiling of the bathroom was lowered and the roof space became a children's room, with the roof lights at the back.

What in section used to be a house of two levels became a house with four levels, with five rooms and no visible changes on the outside except the front door, which was a very subtle one.

Despite the division and all the transformations, somehow the atmosphere and beauty of this house still remains.

These pages: Garden plans gradually implemented over 15 years from 1981.

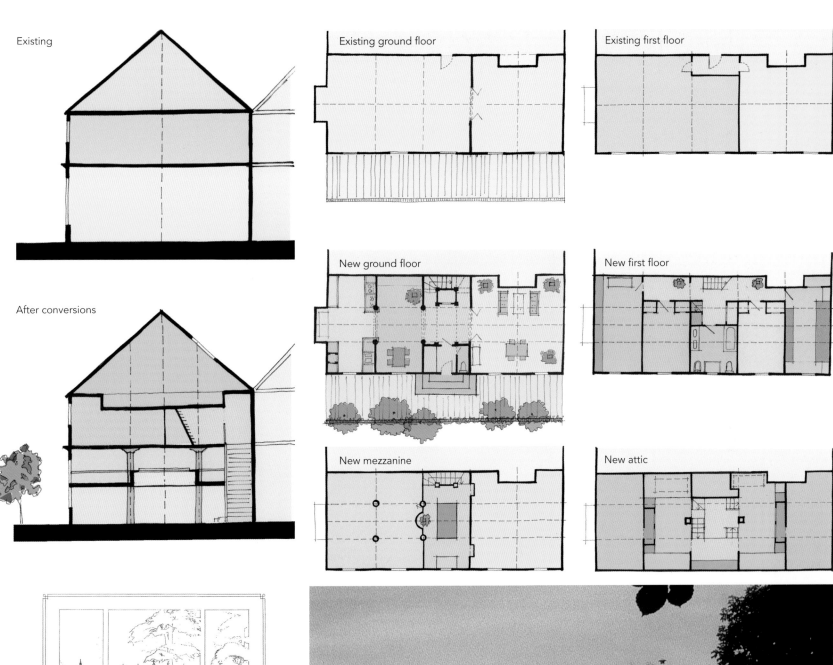

Existing

After conversions

Existing ground floor

Existing first floor

New ground floor

New first floor

New mezzanine

New attic

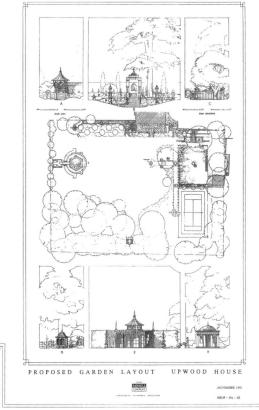

PROPOSED GARDEN LAYOUT UPWOOD HOUSE

Plans for gardens and gazebos Right: Outside front façade

This page and opposite: The main dining and kitchen area; the columns were inserted to support bedroom division walls, creating new bedrooms on the floor above.

Opposite: Lobby ceiling in entrance hallway. This page top: Gallery mezzanine before completion. Bottom: Loft space became the children's bedrooms.

This page: Main bathroom with sea shells. Opposite: The kitchen area is a part of the large volume of the dining area, formerly the house's ballroom.

This page and opposite: The living room area – this was the former 'cardroom'. Sue Farrell was co-designer for much of the interior decoration and furnishings.

This page: Bedroom floor and view out to the garden. Opposite: The decorated hall lobby area.

# Home & Studios, North Marylebone

The city block bounded by Hatton, Boscobel, Penfold and Frampton Streets was originally occupied by terraced houses. Then, between 1920 and 1930, an island block of buildings was erected by Bovis to house a joinery works and furniture factory as an adjunct to their housebuilding division. The different building heights and the external appearance clearly reflect the different stages of the site's development between 1920 and 1940.

In 1940, the Bovis works were requisitioned by the government for the Palmer Aero Works, following the destruction of their Silvertown factory in the Blitz. By 1913 Palmer Aero had made its name by patenting the Palmer Cord Aero tyre and wheel rim – the first pneumatic aircraft tyre not to burst on landing; before its closure in 1984, Palmer Aero manufactured parts for Concorde.

In 1985, Terry Farrell raised a consortium to buy the freehold of the island block with the aim of transforming the site into a mixed-use complex. The conversion reflects an early shift in the concept of the workplace and the re-use of industrial space as studio offices for creative industries; at the same time it brings a lively working community into what was once a rather neglected location.

The freehold was subdivided into several parts: number 9 became known as the Hatton Street Studios, a mix of small companies; number 11 was to house a textile company; number 15 became workshops and storage for an exhibition/events designer; number 17 was transformed into Terry Farrell & Partners' (TFP) new studios and model workshop; and number 19 was taken over by Spitfire Productions' TV company and video editing suite.

During the redevelopment of the block in the mid-1980s, design work concentrated on re-emphasizing the individual character of each building. The 1921 Hatton Street building was extended vertically at the junction with Boscobel Street to create a corner tower for Farrell's own offices, and the whole building was rendered and painted. The 1929 Hatton Street building was extended by two storeys. At street level, the loading doors were replaced by a variety of entrances and shopfronts, unified by decorative tiling. Penfold Street's white rendered façade was preserved and embellished by Babylonian-style rainwater run-off pipes, and towers and balconies were added to mark stair towers and penthouses.

During the late 1990s, as the concept of living and working space continued to evolve, further changes and transformations into loft accommodation and studios began to influence the Palmer Aero buildings. In 1997, TFP vacated number 17 and moved into 7 Hatton Street. What was once a multi-spindle auto shop on the ground floor is now a reception area and meeting rooms, and Palmer's machine shop on the first floor is now a naturally lit architect's studio. The relocation to the ground floor generated a public exhibition space that further animates the street frontage. In Penfold Street, the light wells between the Hatton Street and Penfold Street buildings were opened up as part of the residential conversion, and now make a positive visual contribution to the whole building.

Farrell retained a part of the practice's vacated 17 Hatton Street offices and adapted the rooftop space into a 300-square-metre studio penthouse shown on the following pages. The open volume of the top floor has been planned as a live/work space that stretches from the front to the rear. The design of the studio relies on a continuous accretive process whereby new furniture, some of which is designed by Farrell himself, sits next to modern classics, antiques, model aeroplanes and fish pools.

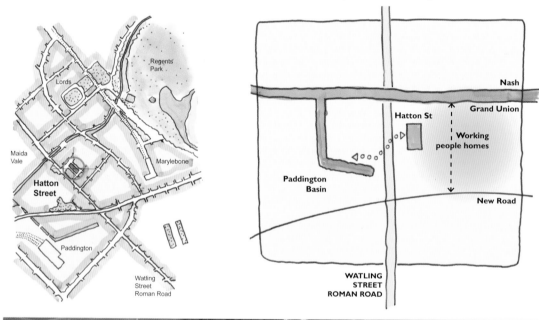

This page: The island site is in a densely populated area of north-west London, surrounded by local authority housing and adjacent to the Edgware Road and Church Street Market.

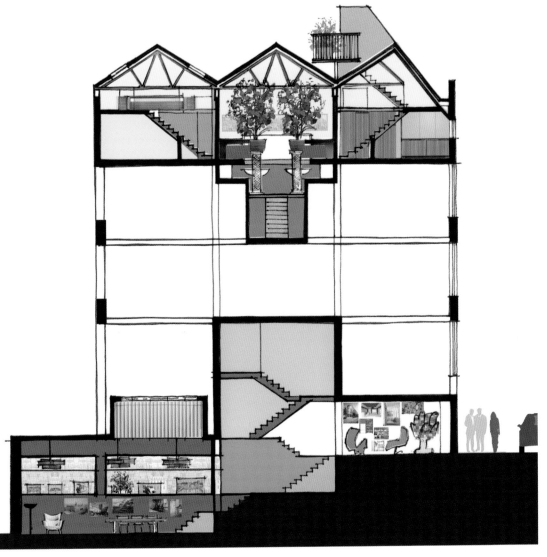

This page: Cross section showing rooftop flat and lower ground floor studio. Regenerated outside facades of offices, studio and home. Before and Neighbourhood Market.

This page top: What is now the living space at the time of the purchase in 1985. Middle: Farrells staff at the time of the purchase. This page bottom: Memories of the former aircraft factory.

Main image: The main living space today.

This page: Views of the penthouse at different stages in its history. Opposite: The penthouse today.

Opposite: Main staircase with recycled fish bowls from Church Street market. This page: Architectural models in the main living areas.

Opposite: The central, top-lit space becomes a garden courtyard/atrium.

This page and opposite: The pictures show the current configuration with the exception of the image top left which shows when the space was a personal work studio.

2

# Gallery & Museum Interiors

Terry Farrell

For a period in the twentieth century, there was 'no history, no context'. The birth of Modernism coincided with the worldwide devastation of place and history – not just due to the two World Wars but also the Russian, Chinese and other revolutions, when the state became all-powerful. During this machine age despotic attempts were made to destroy entire cities – including great historic ones like London, Dresden, Stalingrad, Nanking, Tokyo. Rulers changed from tzars and emperors to new kinds of totalitarian regimes like Mao's that challenged the past and people's shared inheritance of it. In the late 1960s, in probably the most seeping act of destruction anywhere in the twentieth century, all Beijing's gates and walls were demolished; here in the UK, there were post-war plans to demolish much of historic London and provincial cities like Plymouth – not due to war damage but to make them new and modern, to start afresh.

Fifty years later a counter-revolution was well under way. Developments in ecology, anthropology, geology, genetics and DNA have more and more cultivated a sense of place, context and history. Museums, heritage centres in restored buildings, the conservation movement and the depletion of resources have often made re-use more viable than building anew. In both developing countries and the West, museums have become a huge growth industry. Every village, town and city tells its history, restores its buildings and looks at the past and its surviving stories and artefacts as a critical and potent part of the people's present and future.

For me personally, so much of this change began in America – in Philadelphia to be more precise, where as a graduate student I saw the city planners under Ed Bacon restoring and revitalizing the city centre. I read Jane Jacobs on the merits of the traditional non-Modern (non-Corbusian) city and Rachel Carson and our landscape professor Ian McHarg on the wider ecological balance and the harmony of the environment. 'Complexity and contradiction' was very much in the air – Robert Venturi, teaching at the University of Pennsylvania, was writing his book of the same name and married my tutor Denise Scott Brown at this time. Wind forward forty or so years and the changes that took place in the 1970s and 80s have changed everything. Museums as depositories of history and place and indeed the nurturing of our identity, both individually and collectively, are now a rooted part of our culture.

The very narrative of place and history is where it begins. For example, in a modest way, in South Shields on the north-east coast of England, Arbeia Fort, a major Roman supply fort has been unearthed – but the stones are silent without the story of supplies brought from France and southern England to the mouth of the Tyne, or of the Roman wall and Hadrian, its inventor, and of how the wall traversed the whole land mass. I used to walk across a small part of the wall every day – it went through the entrance to our school grounds in Benwell. The Arbeia Fort Museum, like our Centre For Life in Newcastle (2001), has as its first task to take the stories, to recollect and then reconnect them to today, and so establish the narrative that makes these particular museums meaningful. The Centre For Life tells a particular kind of story – one with no historical artefacts – it is a museum of explanation, one where the modern story of genetics, the chemical and biological origins of all creatures, including our own, is told. From Darwin to Crick and Watson, to the modern world of Dolly the sheep. But it is also a site of overlapping architectural narratives – one is of a singular, very fine classical building, a remnant of a cattle market here on the west side of Newcastle designed by north-east England's finest architect John Dobson; another runs through the very threshold, the entrance square to the museum: Newcastle's Scotswood Road, which Geordies have immortalized in song as the route to the Blaydon Races. The cattle market and the Scotswood Road have all gone, but identifying them and celebrating them as we have done brings back, opens up and cements personal, family and community memories. For me, there are personal memories of being a student, as I was here every day in the late 1950s; it was then the major bus station for those travelling westwards and at the time, I lived to the west in the village of Ryton in the Tyne Valley.

This section of the book looks at how our designs for four museums grew from the existing six buildings and their context, and how the explanation and indeed enjoyment of the exhibits relies on layered storytelling, the juxtaposition of different objects, and celebrates richness and complexity. These are definitely not white cubes, not reductionist abstract spaces. I have never held with the view that like objects, society's values – be they in art or historical artefacts – are best set against an anonymous, impersonal background.

Actually, I believe the reverse is true. Most of the best galleries and museums are in old buildings and the more idiosyncratic they are or the more contrast there is in the building narrative, the better. Art, for example, sits well in a power station, a garage or a grand aristocratic house. Similarly, the best are compilations and bundled together in an overlapping way: the Maeght Foundation in southern France, the V&A or Soane Museums in London, or La Piscine in Lille, a gallery from a swimming pool and changing rooms. A generation of curators in the 1950s, 60s and 70s, like the museums' designers and architects, were committed to anonymity, I believe because they wanted to exercise total control over the object, its setting, its reading and context. Such an approach misses so much, and without the revolution of the Postmodern years we would not today have the much greater joy and pleasure and also the serious educational and information side that the historical narrative and context gives our museums and galleries.

The first of these four projects is the Crafts Council building which we designed in 1980–82 for its new location in Waterloo Place at the southern end of London's Regent Street. Crafts are by nature 'impure' and 'diverse'. Craft is universal and eternal – all societies have always made objects from all the different materials man can make things from, and the quality of these objects is timeless – the woven fabrics, vases and mosaics that stretch back millennia are often the equal of the best today. By its nature, craft readily lends itself to a non-Modern ideological approach: the handmade is often the antithesis of the products of the machine age and the two would benefit from joint display in a non-ideological way. So it was a really enjoyable centre to design and enjoyable too to work with all the creative individuals at the Council, and to make a home for it that was not just a gallery but also offices, a café, a library, meeting rooms.

But part of the fascination, both conscious and subliminal, was the setting in a grand, height-of-the-empire classical space and façade, within John Nash's great Regency set-piece of urban planning, surrounded by some of the finest interiors in any city, the clubland of London's Pall Mall. The Nash contribution is spectacular and so sharply relevant to the thesis of this book. If ever Alberti's phrase that the city is like some large house, and the house is in turn like some small city were true, then it is here where Nash began the Prince Regent's route from St James's

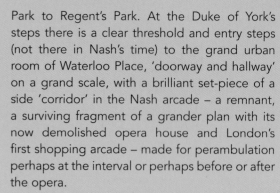

Richness, layering and complexity in museum design.

Left: John Soane Museum, Lincoln's Inn Fields, London
Left below: The Hunterian Museum also on Lincoln's Inn.
The museums sit opposite each other either side of the square. Both are personal lifetime collections, almost contemporaries and yet so different in subject matter: one the inert world of man's artistic artefacts; the other solely organic, the world of biology, species and surgery.

Bottom: The Great North Museum, Newcastle. The exhibition designers were Casson Mann. They created here a twenty-first-century museum display of great character and originality.

Park to Regent's Park. At the Duke of York's steps there is a clear threshold and entry steps (not there in Nash's time) to the grand urban room of Waterloo Place, 'doorway and hallway' on a grand scale, with a brilliant set-piece of a side 'corridor' in the Nash arcade – a remnant, a surviving fragment of a grander plan with its now demolished opera house and London's first shopping arcade – made for perambulation perhaps at the interval or perhaps before or after the opera.

Even without the demolished opera house, there are some great Nash buildings and interiors here – what are now the Institute of Directors and the Haymarket Theatre, both hold set-piece positions: one on a major corner with the great cross street of Pall Mall; the other on the axis with St James's Square – indeed, when the leaves are off the trees in winter, the long cross-axis with St James's Street in the distance is revealed. The Institute of Directors forms one of the southern monumental bookends to Waterloo Place and Pall Mall, opposite it stands the other, the even finer masterpiece of Nash's former pupil Decimus Burton – the Athenaeum. Along the south side of Pall Mall is a string of these private men's clubs; more urban and discreet on the outside but definitely palazzos on the inside as well as the outside. The most complete masterpiece is Charles Barry's Reform Club; The Travellers Club is also by Barry; at the opposite end before St James's Palace is the 1930s RAC Club. These clubs back on to the royal palaces of Clarence House and St James's; there is a social layering from the Mall up to Piccadilly, with the south side of Pall Mall more important than the north, and then up around Piccadilly the streets give way to shops and houses for the middle classes.

Nash's grand route cuts across all these strata, from Waterloo Place with its royal connections, to clubs to banks (including the

one converted to be the Crafts Council) and so on up to Piccadilly and Soho. There is a great connected narrative here, of urban rooms, halls and corridors, and of great buildings and interiors, all linking two gardens – the front and formal one at St James's Park and the 'back' or country end at Regent's Park with its allusions to parkland and the great country houses. It is a kind of hierarchy of London society, both social and physical, all on one street. And the 'as found' interiors of the new Crafts Council derive their place and character from all of this, from setting and context.

The Dean Gallery in Edinburgh (1999) began in matching a new use to a very fine existing building – like Bankside Power Station and Tate Modern, the great architecture came first, and its combinatory effect with its new use became its greatest triumph. As with the Crafts Council, the context of the urban planning defined the whole enterprise. The dense, fortified, medieval Old Town of Edinburgh, sited on a volcanic outcrop, was extended in the eighteenth and nineteenth centuries by its alter ego, the sedate and spacious, classical New Town. On the outskirts of the New Town, in parkland settings were built in a proud but institutional way great classical stone palaces of education – John Watson's School, Stewart's Melville College and Donaldson's Hospital. In 1980 the first was converted into the Scottish National Gallery of Modern Art, with white walls and simplified settings.

Across the road a huge Thomas Hamilton building set in its own parkland had been designed as a home and a school for orphans. A scheme was conceived to convert the empty palace into the 'alternative story of twentieth-century art', as its deputy curator defined it. A story not of clean, clear logical narrative but of the counter-cultures of Art Deco, Dada, Pop Art, Primitivism, Surrealism and eventually Postmodernism, this building is that narrative's architectural reinterpretation. Three permanent collections are juxtaposed here, the Penrose (Surrealism), the Keiller (Dada and Surrealism) and that of the artist Eduardo Paolozzi (1924–2005), one of the pioneers. Temporary exhibition areas form the large second floor; the headquarters and store of the National Galleries of Scotland also occupy spaces in the building, as well as a shop, a café/restaurant and a library and study centre. A substantial amount of architectural energy went into transforming a building designed for enclosure, separation and confinement into one of openness and connection with the outside world. The play between the two contradictions underlies all the work – vistas both open and secret, removed

floors, internal balconies and a vivid backdrop colour scheme set the stage for a visit to a place of sensory delight and richness, an Aladdin's cave, albeit an unsettling and idiosyncratic one. Outside, the landscape and its planning became an important part of the whole experience. New pedestrian crossings linked the road entrance to the two galleries; a new mound and lake was planned and designed jointly with Charles Jencks, secreted and topiaried car parking and pedestrian gates and paths were created to the sculpture in the adjacent graveyard and even to the river itself. Here Antony Gormley subsequently placed figures centre stream down to distant Leith and the docks. Outside, there is room for car parks, allotments and parkland and surprising juxtapositions of connections and functions. It was a gallery design that embraced the widest view of landscape design, masterplanning and interior design.

The Great North Museum (completed 2009) continues this connectivity of urban replanning. This is something that I have been working on for over 25 years in Newcastle, from the Quayside at the bottom of the town to the civic centre at the top. Newcastle's Hancock Museum, which I knew as a boy and forms the basis of the new museum, has a wonderful natural history and ethnological collection. Now the replanned Great Northern Museum has brought the university's two campus museums out to a more public location – the Shefton Museum of Greek Art and Archaeology and the Museum of Antiquities. Brought together it is the assemblage that is the GNM's success, combining what in London would separately be the Natural History Museum, the British Museum and others into one place, existing side by side with wonderfully rich opportunities for linked visual effects and storytelling. Casson Mann, the exhibition designers, were great fun to work with and rightly the museum has been a sensation since it opened.

Much of the design of the architectural interior went into redefining the building and its relationship with the replanning of the town. No longer was the Hancock to be a stand-alone, secluded palace for specialists and hobbyists. The front was opened up with a new lawn, a pedestrian crossing and much-improved access which drives right through all the formerly discrete galleries, linking the whole building vertically and horizontally from front to back. And at the back we built an extension, which has a new entrance onto this central internal hall or 'street'. It is no longer a 'back' but now sits within the overall masterplan as a busy part of the pedestrian campus network.

Finally, a project that we helped redefine – helping to write the brief, organise and plan

the funding and indeed like all enterprises, reinterpret the whole as an historic building – the great 'house of science' on Albermarle Street off Piccadilly – The Royal Institution. The story of this process is as complex and layered as the product of everyone's endeavours. The UK's and particularly London's reinvention of its great institutions, which were born in times of world conquest, exploration, discoveries and empire building, is very recent. Fifty years ago the only thought would have been to demolish, to end an era with formality. Today our era recognises that the layered process of rediscovery has real value in its ability to record and fix in the rebirth of buildings the more open, tolerant, pluralist and impure times that we live in. London in the twenty-first century is no longer the colonies' frontier of captured foreign species but a centre of conservation, as is Kew. The museums of Albertopolis have been reinventing themselves through lottery money. The process of lottery application helps to work through and then openly debate, explore and define the reinterpretation.

The Royal Institution has a long experimental history in the sciences: reflecting its world status as a place where ten chemical elements were discovered and 14 Nobel Prize winners worked was only part of the mission. The main requirement was for the building to project a new openness and accessibility – with a media centre, a café, a bar, restaurants, conference rooms – so that the public could see science as friendly, accessible and not hidden and mysterious. The planform was re-organised to achieve a legible plan for each floor based on a central linking street corridor and a new central atrium with glass lift making a singular vertical connecting point. The exhibition on the lower ground floor contains and explores the scientific story in formal terms, but such was the collection of artefacts found in stores and packing cases that it has been possible to express – in a Soane Museum-like way – the elaborate and beautiful equipment (much of it made on site) as part of an architectural interior of indoor vitrines, linking windows, dividing rooms and even lights and chandeliers. Once it was thought that the only answer for the RI's future was to close the building and move the contents to the Science Museum, but it would have died there – so much is in the bones, the walls and fabric of the building, with its memories and its endless alterations and adaptations and the changes made by so many architects over its long history. The result is a building, a museum and a home of science, itself an extraordinary and unique phenomenon.

# Gallery, St. James

The Crafts Council project demonstrates that the principles of pedestrian organization and hierarchy of space are the same for internal design as for large-scale urban design. For Farrell, a series of interior spaces can be arranged like a small piece of urban design.

The new gallery and information centre for the Crafts Council was built as both a conversion and an extension of their existing premises. The project was to combine the three lower floors of two existing buildings on Waterloo Place, generating a range of public and private spaces, from the public galleries through to the private administration and service areas.

The newly acquired building had a ground-floor level half a metre above the Crafts Council's existing gallery but the mezzanine areas of both premises were on the same level. By repositioning the main entrance between the premises and lowering the level of this new entrance door and reception area, it was possible to form a new entry ramp, which provides easy wheelchair access to the entire ground floor. The central circulation axis from entrance to stair orientated visitors on the gallery floor and directed them through the reception and sales area to the staircase and up to the mezzanine and information centre. The ramp generated the building's main architectural strategy and acted as the central organizer for the whole scheme; it was clearly designed as the most important space in the building, only crossed by a cranked minor access running through the two major gallery spaces.

The Crafts Council also required a new gallery space with a neutral background for the display of objects. The original mouldings and decorations were replaced by larger mouldings, and blank white wall spaces were created where possible above a common skirting line, which formed a plinth to the counter, bookshelf and other elements in the lower-floor areas. The subtle patterning in the new timber flooring worked with the modified ceilings to define sub-spaces within the two single-storey galleries. The suspended ceiling of the higher space of the original gallery was removed, revealing a splendid and ornate strap-moulded plaster ceiling. New fibrous plaster columns flanked the principal axes; a storage unit, reception desk and bookshelves defined the reception and sales area, and the geometry of the linoleum flooring was designed to respond to the various activities along its length. At mezzanine level, the removal of part of the wall dividing the two mezzanines allowed the introduction of a set of slide-display cases to create views back down into the gallery below.

Creating an internal identity and finding a visual language that reconciled the different characteristics of the two historically listed Victorian interiors were the main difficulties. For Farrell, the nature of the small *objets d'art* and crafts to be displayed demanded a setting with a sense of place. Yet the most public space, and that which was the main focus of design attention within the scheme, was not the gallery space itself, but the areas between: the circulation space and the route that connected all the spaces. The relationship between these spaces was heightened by opening up the first floor with overlooking balconies and views into the restaurant so that the whole sequence of spaces was interlinked.

This hierarchy within the interior of the building, the miniature street ordering the lesser spaces, was designed to relate to Waterloo Place, which formed part of Nash's hierarchy of spaces along the triumphal route from Carlton House to Regent's Park. As such, both this scheme and that for Lloyds Bank, responded to and formed part of the urban structure of the area, which connects Nash's exterior spaces – defined by imposing street façades – to the grand entrance halls and public rooms found in the London clubs. Behind the set piece façade, the Crafts Council building mirrored the world of clubland – a great sequence of spaces where members meet and socialize, united by a common interest or purpose.

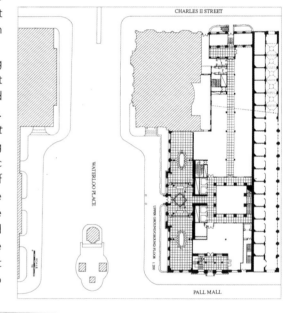

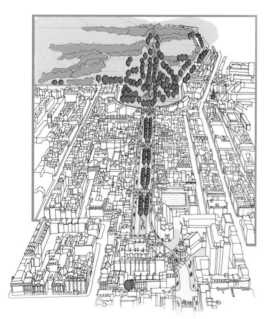

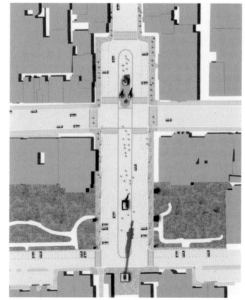

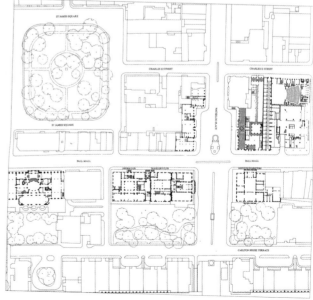

Bottom left and middle: View up Portland Place to Regent's Park and Waterloo Place and Lower Regent's Street enhancement scheme. Both images are part of Farrell's vision for the Nash Ramblas, to rediscover the route of Nash's masterplan. Top right: Ground floor plan of bank building proposals. Bottom right: Nolli plan of Crafts Council and surroundings.

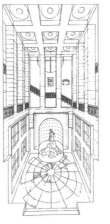

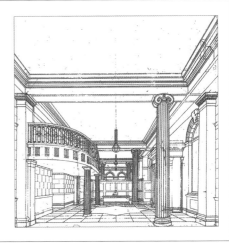

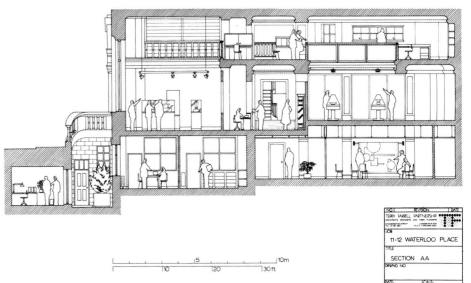

SECTION AA

11-12 WATERLOO PLACE

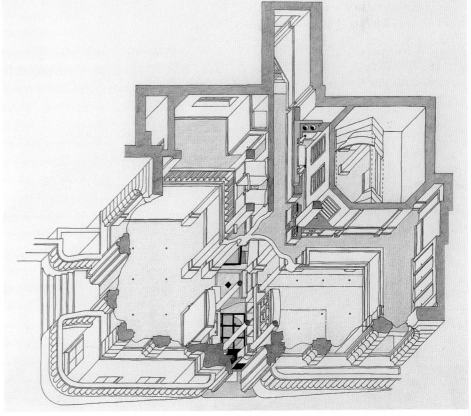

Top row: Farrell interior scheme for new hotel and in bank premises. Bottom left: Grand entrance to existing Crafts Council building. Middle: Cross-section Crafts Council.
Bottom right: Axonometric of ground floor galleries.

These pages: Views of the previous exterior and interior of the building and (in colour) new interiors.

This page: View from bookshop looking towards staircase leading to slide index and café. Opposite: Gallery Number One.

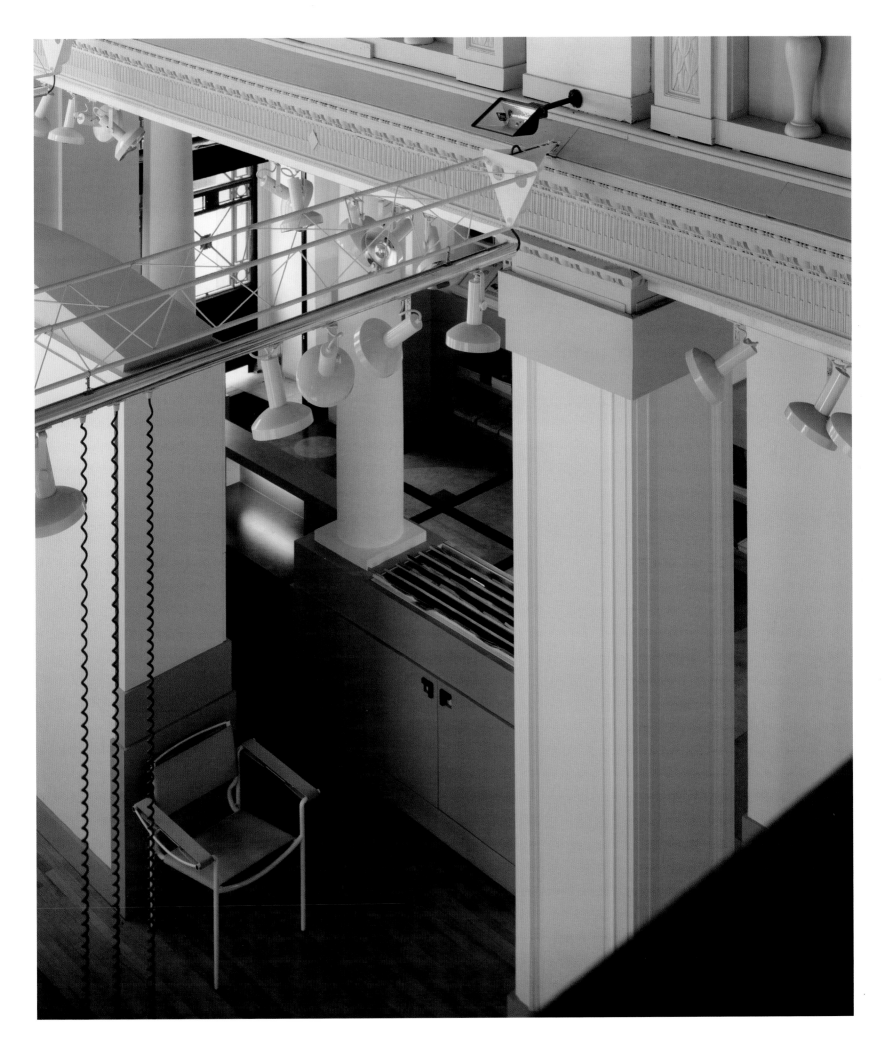

This page: Existing slide cabinets were placed on balconnettos overlooking the gallery below.  Opposite: New doorway and inlaid vinyl flooring.

Top and main image: The café area, the chairs were specially designed by Fred Baier. This page bottom: Gallery Number Three.

# Modern Art Galleries, Edinburgh

Before starting the redesign of Thomas Hamilton's three-storey Grade A-listed Dean Orphanage into a visionary exhibition space, TFP were required to transform the landscape into an appropiate setting for an art gallery. The gallery is located in close proximity to the existing Gallery of Modern Art. The resulting masterplan created an arts campus, incorporating both buildings in a unified parkland setting of landscaped gardens and sculpture designed in collaboration with Charles Jencks. This design provides the visitor with a synthesis of art and nature that emphasizes the contrast between the grid layout of Edinburgh's Old Town and the attractiveness of the New Town.

Hamilton's building, using the typology of the English country house, was a narrow 'H' block with projecting pavilions on both sides. The austere interiors were in direct contrast to the exuberant exterior, with its Baroque-inspired towers, which used to function as stairwells and chimney stacks.

The primary task was to resuscitate the inside of the building, bringing the quality of the exterior into the interior spaces. This was achieved by placing mixed objects in areas of the building other than the galleries and by using motifs from past and present to establish an architectural discourse and to reflect the work of Thomas Hamilton and Sir John Soane. The main difficulty was the development of a functional plan within the constraints of the building's Grade A listing. Extracting a rich and layered cultural and historical narrative from it, TFP aimed to stimulate the senses with a clever interplay between juxtaposition, games playing and historical context.

The plan was organized around three key elements: the four corner pavilions, the twin stair towers and the central 'temple' front. It was divided into the basement storage, the administration facilities in the wings and the public exhibition spaces in the central section – four rooms joined vertically by the double-height hall and by the stairs in the towers, and horizontally by a central corridor. This central corridor, painted in deep blue, is key to the design; running north-south along the central axis of the gallery, it provides views into the two stair towers that lead to each wing, the gallery floor above and to the galleries, café and shop.

The Dean Art Gallery replaces the much-used 'white-box' formula with clearly delineated boundaries, both physically and metaphorically.

An intense arrangement of colours and materials is used and a series of Surrealist-inspired spaces have been designed using devices that aim to intrigue: mirrors and enfilade doors, wall breaks, surprise portholes, changes of level and a dramatic double-height space filled with a 9-metre-high sculpture. There is no consistency of size or ceiling height, and colour and lighting effects are used to define spatial parameters.

The gallery itself and its suggestive architecture become participants in the exhibit, communicating particular impressions and surprising the visitor with never-ending ways of looking – an important theme in Surrealist thinking. The circulation spaces as well as the exhibition spaces are all about sensory experience.

Farrell has always been interested in the alternative, and the experience of the Dean Art Gallery is a clear example of this: an old building where there is a sensation of the history of things and where an ordered plan is used to reflect an alternative view of art and architectural history. The result is an experience that neatly combines architecture, landscape and sculpture, using harmonious and unified spaces and artworks, and a complex variety of routes. The buildings and the landscape are enhanced by the artworks. The architecture is barely perceived; it seems merely to be part of the original building's process of growth. It does not reflect an agenda that reads as either rational or modernist – it is a complete world of its own.

This page: Aerial view of The Dean and its surroundings.

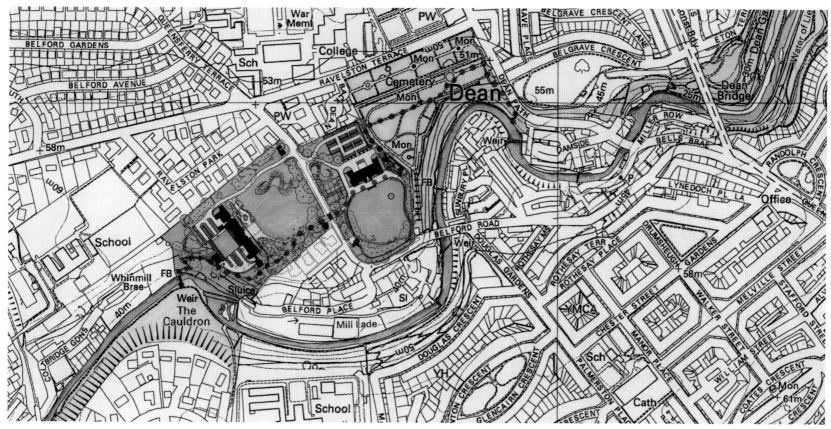

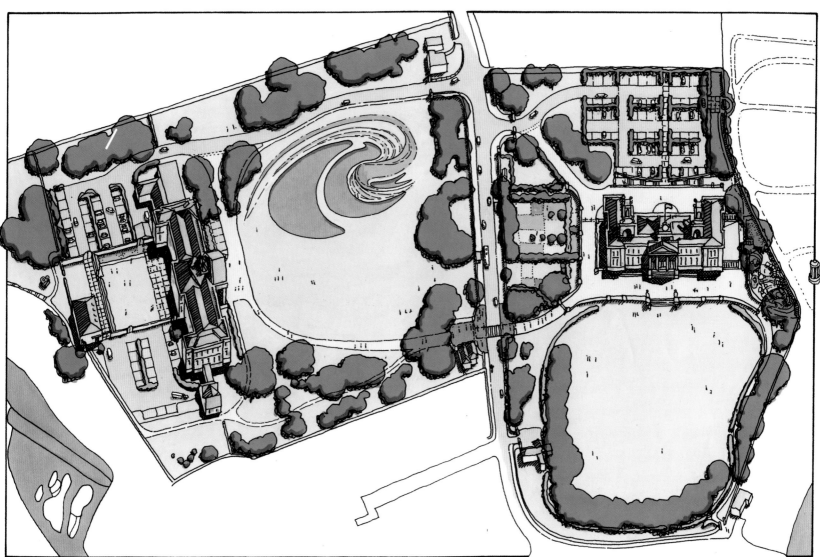

Top: Location plan showing the building's fit within the bend of the Water of Leith. Bottom: Masterplan drawing.

Top: Long section showing the vertical and horizontal continuity. Bottom: Cross-section.

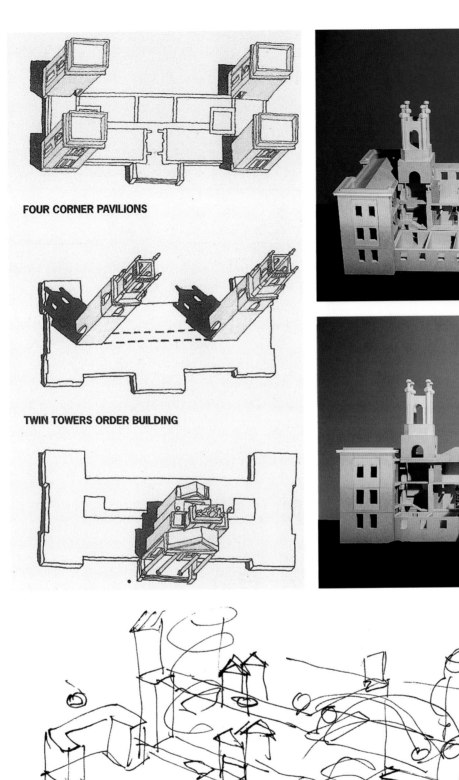

**FOUR CORNER PAVILIONS**

**TWIN TOWERS ORDER BUILDING**

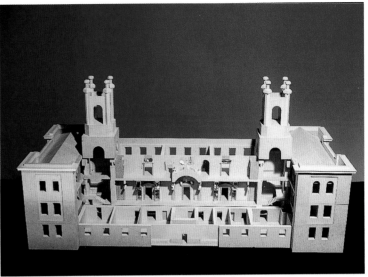

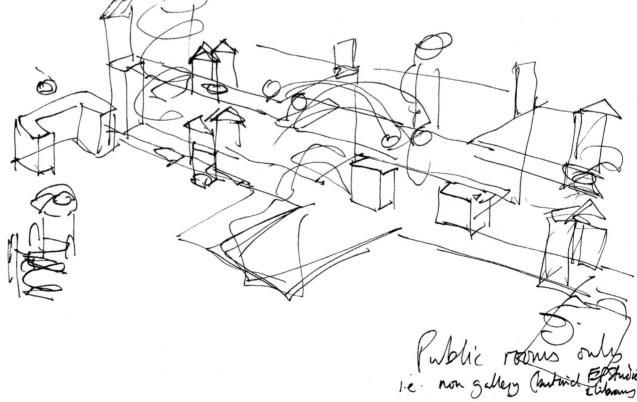

Public rooms only
i.e. non gallery (not incl. E.P. Studio & Library)

Bottom: Concept sketch by Farrell to work out and explain the interconnectedness and opening up of the once cellurarized interiors.

Bottom left: 3D land sculpture in grounds, designed by Charles Jencks and Terry Farrell. Middle and bottom right: The interiors before alteration work.

This page: Ground floor main axis corridor.

Top left: The shop – a gallery in its own right. Top right and bottom: The Keiller Library.

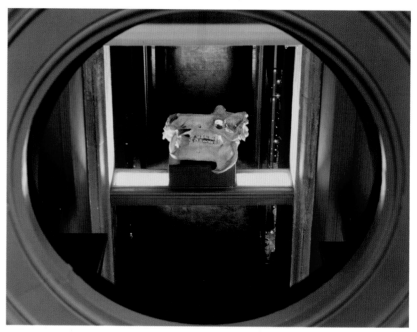
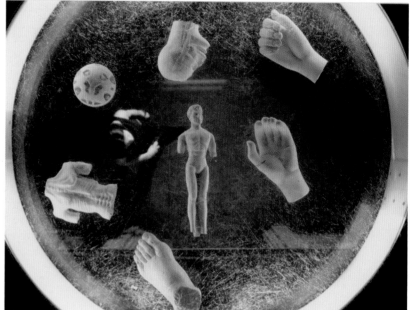

These pages: Every opportunity was taken to create linking views – new glazing view points in floors, walls and cabinets connect to rooms and floors beyond.

These pages: Sculptures by Eduardo Paolozzi, his studio/living space was permanently recreated in the gallery (see page 93).

Top left: Recreation of Paolozzi's studio. Bottom: Tiling and cloakroom designed by Sue Farrell.

# 'The Home of Science', Piccadilly

The Royal Institution was founded to carry out research and introduce science to broader society. It is the oldest and one of the most prestigious scientific establishments in the world.

The RI is located in a row of Grade I-listed Georgian townhouses within the Mayfair conservation area. The RI took over these houses and converted them into one building. Over time, the many layers, additions and reconfigurations of the internal spaces had created a largely incoherent building with inefficient use of space and very poor circulation.

TFP were appointed as masterplanners and lead designers for its restoration, refurbishment and subsequent emergence as a 'salon for science'. The prestigious Albermarle Street facility is centrally located, with good links to transport. The overall objective was to achieve a radical conversion and adaptation of the building to provide dynamic, extensive new facilities for a wider audience, promoting social inclusion at this world-class institution.

One of the key design principles was to make the building much more accessible to the public. As well as rationalizing the circulation and providing deep views into the building from street level, TFP aimed to reinstate all the heritage rooms, creating a high-quality masterplan for the building. Where possible, these rooms were restored using like-for-like materials and colour palettes. While the heritage colours and materials used have been reinterpreted in a contemporary way, a clear distinction can nevertheless be drawn between these rooms and the new spaces. Glass and stainless steel has been used in the new atrium area to juxtapose with the existing design, and this glazing allows daylight to pour into the rear of the building, which was previously dark and oppressive. To improve general circulation, each floor has a central corridor spine with level or low-level ramped access.

Apart from the existing exhibition space in the basement, the building itself did not tell a story; it did not reflect the richness of its history. The mission of the RI was explained in the extended exhibition areas and by using the whole fabric of the building to show its collection of paintings and drawings. Displaying objects and telling the stories behind the artefacts led to a complete rethink of the basement exhibition area.

All of the interventions and improvements to the building were carried out in a way that kept the best of what was already there. It was possible to create this new environment without destroying the principle parts because so much of it was hidden away from the public as storage and back rooms. The masterplan emphasized the functional relation between the building's parts and its whole, which was instrumental in establishing a new vision for the Royal Institution. The RI is now reconfigured, not as a museum but as a living, working, lively and engaging institution, which will inspire an enthusiasm for science in future generations in a state-of-the-art venue where everyone can feel at home.

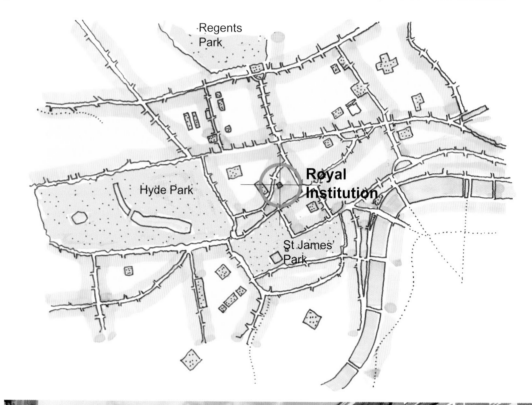

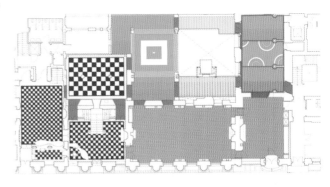

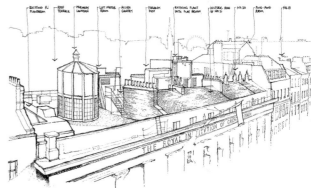

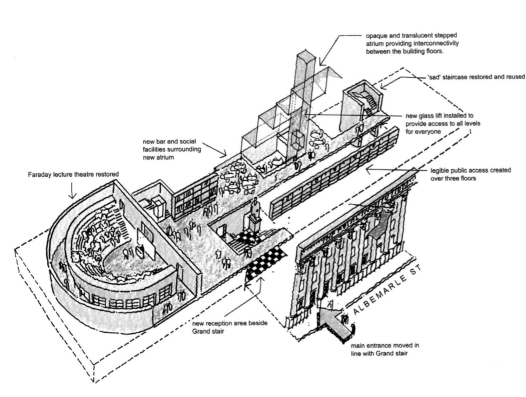

opaque and translucent stepped atrium providing interconnectivity between the building floors.

'sad' staircase restored and reused

new glass lift installed to provide access to all levels for everyone

new bar and social facilities surrounding new atrium

legible public access created over three floors

Faraday lecture theatre restored

new reception area beside Grand stair

main entrance moved in line with Grand stair

ALBEMARLE ST

Top left: Exploded axonometric of existing building. Bottom left: Plan of proposed interventions. Top right: Photos of existing interiors. Right second from top: Rooftop remodelling and extensions. Right third from top: Ground floor plan. Bottom: Model showing ground floor.

Opposite: The main entrance hallway with statue of Michael Faraday. This page: Grade 1-listed, historic interiors were restored but added to.

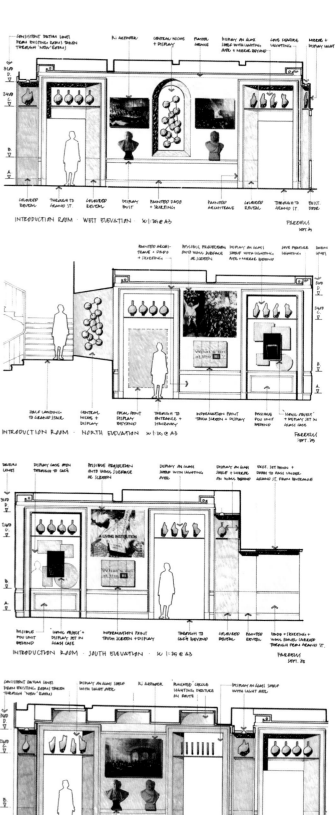

Top and right: The 'Introduction Room' begins the narrative – with artefacts from the archives integrated into architectural features.

Opposite and top left and right: The new restaurant dining room and bar  This page centre and bottom: The lower ground floor exhibition area – display design by Event Communications.

Opposite bottom right and this page: The restored main auditorium with improved seating, lighting and environmental control.

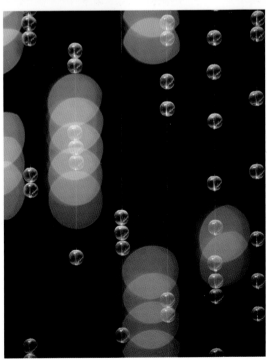

Opposite: The new atrium. This page top left: Street entrance to Time and Space bar. Top right: View from atrium to reception and café area. Middle left: Re-found scientific objects originally hidden in storage and now used as decoration. Middle right: View from atrium to reception and café area. Bottom row: Once forgotten stairwell at rear of building now used by the public to access exhibition area.

# Museum Regeneration, Newcastle

The essence of the Great North Museum project in Newcastle was a commitment to opening up and connecting places and spaces, and collections and history. The museum's original Hancock Building was designed by John Wardle in 1878. It occupies an elevated position at the northern entrance to the city centre, on the edge of the Newcastle University campus.

TFP was commissioned first in 1991 to re-imagine Newcastle's riverside and again in 2000 to re-plan Newcastle University's campus on the north side of the city and integrate it with a cultural quarter anchored by the Great North Museum. Building on this strategy, Farrells proposed another large-scale plan: a linear route – a promenade fancifully dubbed 'the Geordie Ramblas' – linking this emerging cultural quarter to the Millennium Bridge, following existing routes for 3 kilometres uphill to the museum site.

Newcastle University now has a dominant presence at the uphill northern gateway to the city. The new museum combines the university's own archaeological collections with the Hancock Museum's historic collections in spaces that are no longer inward and contained. Opening up and connecting views and visitor paths juxtaposes old and new architectural interventions, as well as ethnological, archaeological and natural history displays. The result is a kind of miniature version of several grand London museums, combined in one cohesive place.

Set north--south within a compact plateau raised above the street and surrounded by mature trees, the Grade II-listed building was originally a specialized building with dedicated rooms; each gallery was self-contained and accessed from the perimeter. Now, large ashlar-clad openings allow passage through and into the new build.

The primary architectural interventions were to clear away and re-landscape the frontage, visually reconnecting the museum to the city centre. A new front was built to the rear with a new extension building that consolidates the pedestrian routes of the university masterplan. Internally, the axis from the civic centre to the statue of university founder William George Armstrong to the entrance portico is extended inwards into a long vista path, which runs right through the building to the new extension and pedestrian walkway beyond. Side aisles and first-floor balconies were similarly opened up, so that not just axial but diagonal cross-views provide an interacting visual framework, which the exhibition design capitalizes on.

The extension is separated visually and physically from the Hancock building by a double-height 'galleria'. Alongside its circulatory function, the galleria allows the identity and form of the museum buildings to be read clearly against the large-scale university blocks that surround them.

The new building manages to stand its ground. Its entire north elevation, in fact, has a lab-like quality suited to the campus context, enforced by the panellized roof that curves into the balcony. The flexible first-floor gallery is large and can be subdivided into three parts. On the ground floor, the museum's central route leads through a café and into the plaza, which doubles as a university through-route. Glazed doors at either end of the galleria lead into the landscaped grounds of the plateau. It is refreshing to be able to enter and exit the museum in so many ways; people swarming everywhere make the building feel porous.

TFP's sensitive refurbishment, clear planning, multiple through-routes and finely calibrated extension suggest an approach to place-making that could transform the entire city. The proposed 'Ramblas' route now has something tangible and attractive, contextual and modern at its beginning and its end. TFP's goal was to orchestrate the relationships between place, history and new city-making, with architecture and interior design continuing in an ever increasing scale, from the details of display exhibits to internal and external streets to gardens and highways beyond. The design is both Victorian and modern, but the concept is culturally Postmodern, embracing both complexity and contradiction.

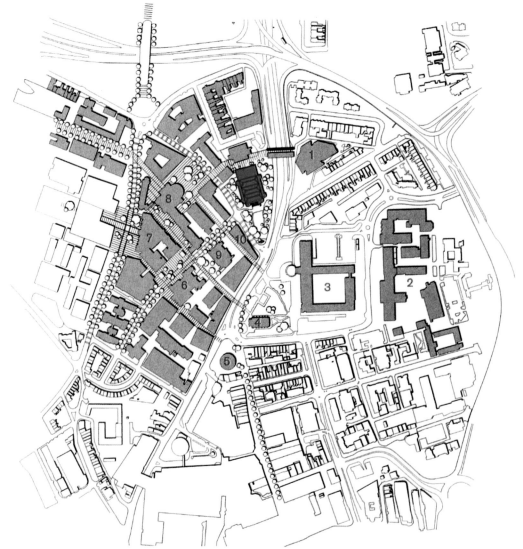

**University and Cultural Quarter Masterplan**
1. Robinson Library  2. Northumbria University  3. Civic Centre  4. St Thomas' Church  5 Haymarket metro station
6. Refectory/students' union  7. King's Hall  8. Hatton Gallery  9. Playhouse  10. Allied cultural uses

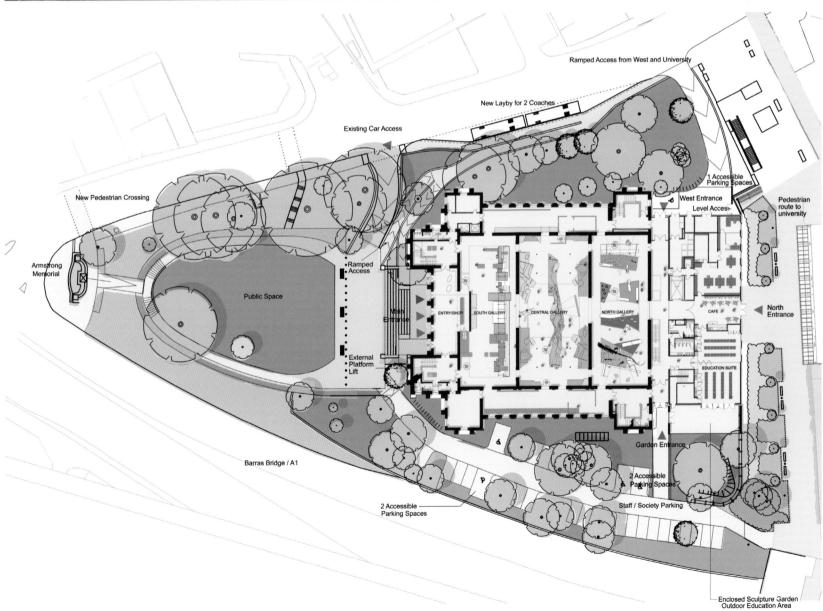

Top left: Rejuvenated building façade. Top right: the new extension sits beside the existing building and large-scale university buildings. Bottom: Site plan.

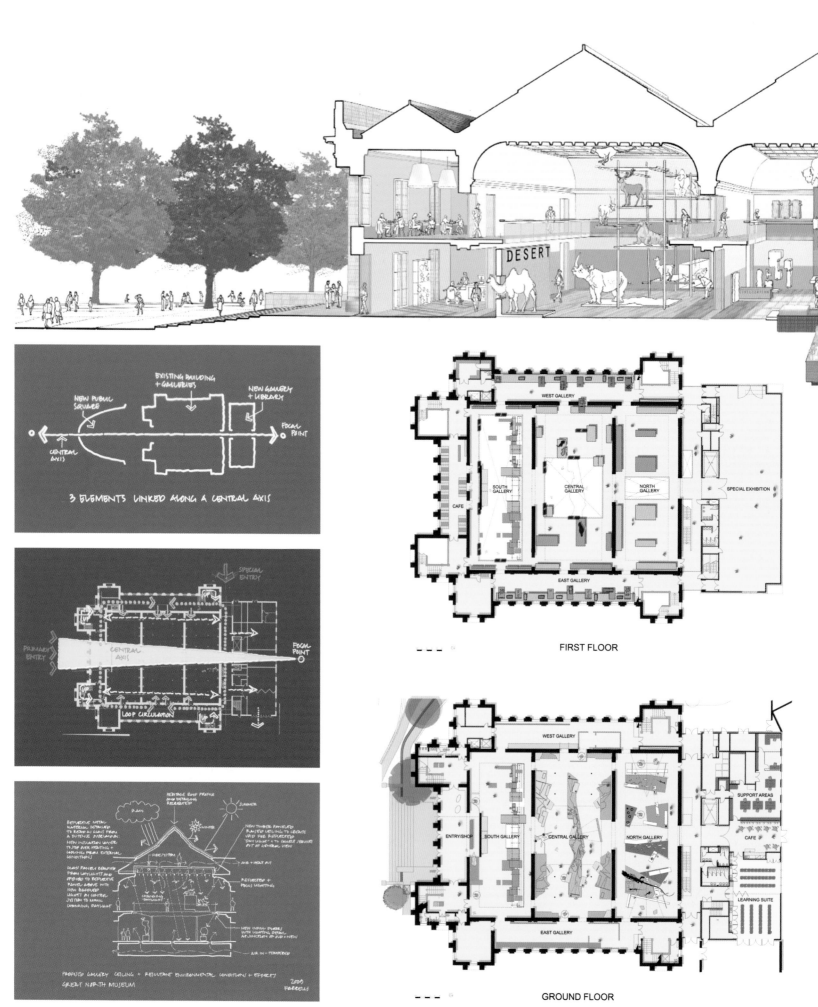

Top: Illustrative concept section. Left: Diagrams showing connectivity. Right: Ground and first floor plans.

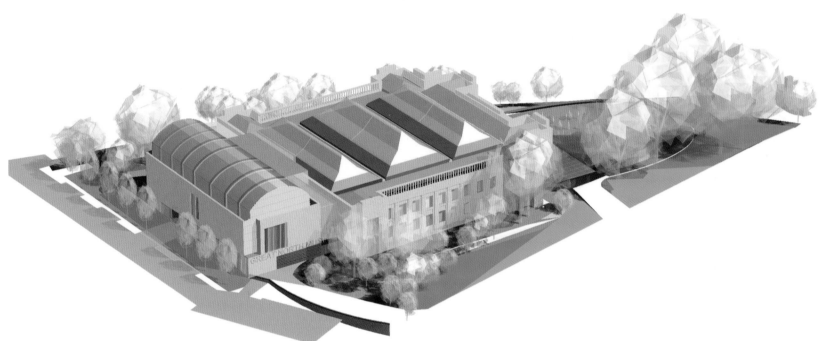

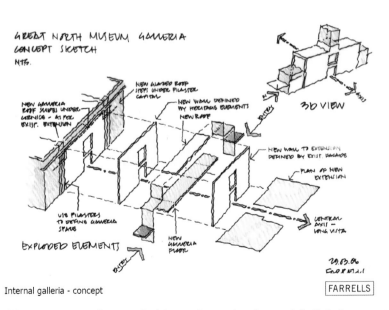

GREAT NORTH MUSEUM GALLERIA
CONCEPT SKETCH
NTS.

3D VIEW

NEW GLAZED ROOF STEPS UNDER PILASTER CAPITAL

NEW GALLERIA ROOF SLOPES UNDER CORNICE - AS FOR EXIST. EXTENSION

NEW WALL DEFINED BY HERITAGE ELEMENTS

NEW ROOF

NEW WALL TO EXTENSION DEFINED BY EXIST. FACADE

PLAN OF NEW EXTENSION

CENTRAL AXIS - LONG VISTA

USE PILASTERS TO DEFINE GALLERIA SPACE

EXPLODED ELEMENTS

NEW GALLERIA FLOOR

Internal galleria - concept

FARRELLS

Middle: Axonometric of existing building and extension. Bottom left: Galleria concept sketch. Bottom right: Model of extension.

This page bottom right: Earlier Victorian exhibition space. Opposite: New exhibition area, display by Casson Mann.

This page and opposite bottom: New openings now link existing halls.

This page top: Inside the new extension with temporary exhibition space.

This page: There are four restored stone staircases, each situated at a corner of the existing building.

This page and opposite: The reinterpretation of the existing halls. Opposite bottom: Inside the new extension circulation areas.

This page: Existing halls reinterpreted and linked together. Opposite: Existing mezzanine level with retained balcony and balustrade.

# 3

# Workplace Interiors

Terry Farrell

If the Modernist tradition of the twentieth century saw the house as a machine for living in, then it was clear that the office was a machine for working in. And yet, there are several different ways of interpreting this basic Modernist concept.

It was of course readily apparent in the post-war commercial office buildings, in the big 1950s New York skyscrapers, the Lever Building (1951–2) by SOM and Mies van der Rohe's Seagram Building (1954–8) – the office box as a functional machine had arrived with its clear floor, big span, the most compact and best-organized lift and service core, escape stairs, fire strategy and cladding systems. All of this became a mechanized artefact that truly began to represent the city of the mid-twentieth century. And yet, this specialist twentieth-century building type had begun in a more complex way. As a student I visited Frank Lloyd Wright's Larkin Building in Buffalo (1904) and his Johnson Wax Headquarters Building (1936–39 and 1944) in Racine, Wisconsin. Both were extraordinarily visual and unique, and combined spatial drama, visual character and particularized detailing, colours and expression, and also represented a growing phenomenon for the office building type in that the building itself was a corporate advert and an iconic expression of the personality of the company itself. The conical, dripping, wax-like forms of Lloyd Wright's masterpiece in particular, referenced Johnson's role as manufacturers of wax products.

After World War II, the anonymous box increasingly became the norm for the office building and was adopted for both the corporate owner/occupier, such as Seagram and Lever, but also for the commercial/speculative office building which became ubiquitous in the capital cities of commerce like New York, London, Hong Kong and Tokyo. Inevitably there followed an interior furnishing and interior design philosophy that matched these context-free, entropic spaces and in the 1960s and 70s it was universally known as 'Bürolandschaft' (office landscape). With it grew a whole methodology of organizing office planning, 'space management'. Two of its proponents in the UK were fellow students and friends of mine Frank Duffy and John Worthington. A philosophy and method of work lifestyle was coupled with Bürolandschaft and with an office furniture type derived from systems such as that of Herman Miller. All this combined to provide a process-driven, universal solution applicable to all offices, all companies, all types of work and all kinds of buildings.

I became fascinated by this universality of workplace space utilization and flexible furniture design. The furniture trolley unit I designed for a student hostel in Bayswater, London 1968 (which was admired on a trip to Britain at the time by Buckminster Fuller) pioneered many of the principles shown in Herman Miller's flexible furniture system. So when my then partner Nicholas Grimshaw and I obtained our first proper office and more permanent home at Paddington Street, Marylebone, we fitted it out with Herman Miller even though the space was fairly confined and was by no means an open, generalized entropic one. It was the back of a showroom, and a fairly contorted space at that, but with flexible overhead tubes bringing the wiring down in any location, the office workstations within the Bürolandschaft free-form plan, it became our workplace home.

I've always been fascinated by how Frank Duffy and John Worthington and their company DEGW developed a relationship cross-over between this study of interior space, and the work lifestyle it addressed, and urban planning. Both are a kind of space and place management; the end spectrums of the continuum. Both follow what Alberti expressed – 'the city is like some large house and house is in turn like some small city'. By straddling architecture in the middle, a link was made at each end, which I have found useful in my own work, between the insides of buildings and outdoor public spaces, between the interior rooms and the big 'rooms' of cities and the public realm.

After my partner of 15 years Nicholas Grimshaw had left the practice in 1980 to set up his own office, we began to reform our own offices at Paddington Street. I started dismantling what we had and began again within the same office space. From the start I took it as a given to keep the Herman Miller that had resource value and I re-used the furniture as 'found' objects. I saw this as an opportunity to cannibalize and reinterpret it in more fixed spaces with spatial particularity and identity. I wrote an essay in *AA Quarterly* at the beginning of the 1970s on the difference between Buckminster Fuller's statement that change is normal and Louis Kahn's that the fundamentals of a building are what it wants to be, that both the ever-changing and the fundamentalist, monumental static could often lead to the same conclusion. I took the Herman Miller and decided to study what exactly were the real fundamentals of the space. However flexible it was, was there a reposed singular arrangement of preferred permanence? This led to the discovery of a hierarchy that reflected almost an urban plan: instead of sprinkling the furniture freely we now had a street, a central route right from the front to the back: we had areas dedicated to specialist things, we had a leisure area outside that became a beach, a fun area; there was the permanent kitchen and dining space attached to its plumbing; there was a meeting room area and of course there were also workspaces.

The conclusion at that time was that the workspaces had never really been varied in the Bürolandschaft era: they had stayed static anyway, because there were a limited number of workstation designs and the idea that you were continuously taking it down and putting it up again was illusory. Indeed those who did undertake to deconstruct and rebuild often got into difficulties losing parts – where did you store the extra bits, and where did you get the new ones? In the end the idea of constantly changing space and furniture was completely impracticable, so we looked for the fixed; and indeed the personal workspace – the workstation as it had been called – became a real place, a place which the individual would sit in and occupy like his or her home, to which the individual committed large parts of his or her life, designing buildings, working in an architect's office. Even the components were given a greater sense of hierarchy and expression: the filing cabinet centre became almost a piece of art, a sculpture in the entrance hall; and we characterized the surplus of flexible wiring in an almost monumental way by associating it with a parade of lights, almost like street lights that went down a central passageway or street.

It was at this time that I began to take an interest in urban planning and became engaged in a debate between 'designed' Modernist city planning and more natural organic city planning. All my life I had felt passionately that whatever the merits of Modernist architecture, these merits did not apply to city planning. Modernist buildings work as much as they do in the city context by juxtaposition. They need an old city as a contrast, like the Pompidou Centre does in Paris or the London Eye on the South Bank. It is almost as if they work as surreal, displaced objects; the traditional city is maintained, even reinforced, by its renegade presence.

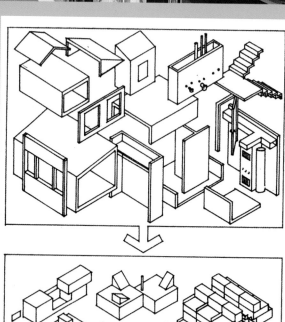

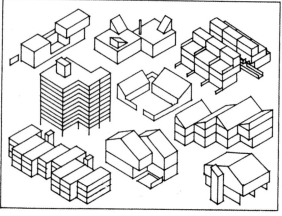

Left and below left: Contemporary workplace designs by Clive Wilkinson who once worked in the TFP office. The images show 'urban village' workplace interiors within large sheds, Silicone Valley, US.

Below right: 1970s drawings by Ezra Ehrenkrantz. Some designers were already exploring mass production's potential for creating complexity and choice rather than standardization.

The debate I became engaged with, a very public one at the time, was over Mies van der Rohe's proposed tower for Peter Palumbo at Mansion House Square (designed in 1967), which was being championed by Richard Rogers over a decade after Mies' death. I accepted the invitation by Save and English Heritage to produce an alternative scheme which kept all the existing fine Victorian buildings. I presented and appeared at a public enquiry, and in due course we won. The alternative scheme reflected the tradition of the shape and form of the city. Colin Rowe's *Collage City* was very much in my mind as I examined the principles of Mies' Modernist proposal – a single object and a single space to replace a whole complex of buildings with courtyards, streets and historic relationships, with many front doors, a richness of expression and variety that was quite extraordinary within this major high street in the City of London.

It's fascinating how the main street 'Cheapside', the City's high street, is now being reclaimed as the heart of the city, not just as a shopping street but as the kind of mixed-use street that I proposed. In the early 1980s when I was fighting the campaign on Mansion House, it was the test case for the City's politicians and businessmen who wanted to demonstrate that the City of London could become almost an urban business park with large, square, tall, massive, efficient Modernist tower blocks marching across the whole of its landscape. Now of course richness and variety 'placemaking' are seen as an asset. The real competition, they realised, comes from office space in really composed places, planned from the outset as 'places', like Canary Wharf and the joining boroughs, and particularly the West End of London. They all have 'place' to offer, while the City spent so many decades trying to destroy 'place' in the interests of no place and Modernist efficiency. The large-scale masterplan of the Mies tower at Mansion House and its so-called plaza in front of it also became the test case for a shift towards a greater interest in interiors and the possibility for 'place' and space-making within the office itself.

At that time I received a commission from a new television studio. It was an opportunity I could not miss and led to one of the most enjoyable enterprises I have been involved with. It was for a breakfast television start-up called TV-am. From the outset this was an opportunity to create an identity through a building. It was going to have a very powerful existence on screen, a virtual reality existence, but as it turned out it would also have an opportunity to have a powerful presence within a run-down area of London next to some prime industrial artefacts

of canals and railway warehouses, and to act as a catalyst for regeneration of the area. It would have a physical presence that was a landmark, becoming the symbol for a newly vibrant district of London.

It was of course essentially a populist television station. It was commercial TV, aimed at entertainment (or 'edu-tainment') and led by major television celebrities like Michael Parkinson, Anna Ford, David Frost and Peter Jay. All these people wanted a building inside and out that had a vibrant and strong personality, that was a fun place to work in, and that really expressed in all its parts in every sense what life was – that work was not a drudge, was not a product solely of efficiency but a product of rewarding teamwork, of creativity, of life and colour.

In one go, we were able to put aside the purity and efficiency of the office building as a factory and replace it with something quite new. This is not to say that a lot of it was not based on an underlying business-like approach. In fact we ourselves found the building, negotiated its purchase, arranged for a design/build contractor to deliver it and eventually created a new television building which was in technical terms one of the most up to date and often thought of as the best of its time. It is now the main European studios of MTV. All of this was designed and delivered in something close to 21 months and for an extraordinarily low budget price. I was once challenged by a City banker at a reception who said to me: 'You know, they made a mistake letting you build such an expensive building – it's not good for business.' I then pointed out that actually it was two-thirds the budget of any normal television station that had been built before. He paused and then said, 'Well then, what you've done has made it look expensive and that's not good for business either.'

Like our own offices it was an act of cannibalization and reinterpretation and transformation, all of which was a far cry from the *tabula rasa* 'designed object' of fundamentalist Modernism. Here we were dealing with collage, with layering, with juxtaposition but also with storytelling and image-making. The old warehouse and factory was kept for the most part and indeed gave shape and inspiration to the final product. The front wall is virtually the only new element. I saw front, middle and back as having three separate and distinct architectural programmes – all very different from each other and of course, different again from Modernism, where purity and particularly consistency of expression were seen as paramount and where the singularly designed object with attributable singular authorship were critical.

The process itself I found fascinating. The brief for the architecture and the interior design could not be written until the on-air programme was defined. What happened in the studio, what the programme delivered was the starting point for the whole enterprise and its on-air expression – the direction, the technical areas, the green rooms, the office, the news rooms, the staff quarters, staff numbers and so on all flowed from what happened on screen.

The blurring of the use of areas was something that I was to develop in art galleries – the shop and the café at Edinburgh's Dean Gallery (1999) became like galleries in themselves. Similarly the staff areas, the staircases at TV-am had the potential to become television studios, and so very soon after completion the cameras came out and were filming the on-air show, not just in the studios but on the canal bank and in the staff café and particularly on the central atrium staircase. This space was planned as the focus of the spatial organization because the whole building, although only two storeys high, was over 30 metres deep and the atrium was glazed above by the factory roof lights, which brought light to the centre of the plan (just as it did in the factory from a similar date which became my home on Hatton Street).

We immediately followed TV-am with another television studio – this time in Docklands, East London. Again it was a radical refurbishment – this time of a concrete-framed banana warehouse. The planform was able to follow the discipline of the well-built original building and a light-touch design approach ensured that the gutsy solid presence of the building always, as it were, glowered through the lighthearted TV studio add-ons. The building was demolished after only a few years to make way for Canary Wharf.

TV-am, Limehouse Studios and the TFP offices were all places that dealt with the owner-occupier, but shown here are also examples of the speculative or commercial workplace. These are more abstract and involve the planning of interiors to be used by unknown occupants. We have tended to work with a certain type of project, one which is anchored in an urban environment where the context is complex, making places and spaces both around the building in urban design terms and inside the building as a kind of interior urbanism. Interior urbanism is key to much of this book, as internal and external urbanism are interlocked in so many of the projects we've done.

At Charing Cross Station (1990–91), we masterplanned a wide area, it was a truly urban project. It began with the external public corridor of Villiers Street, which was completely re-arranged and partially paved so that it became a front door, a local high street for people and not a street for traffic. The big public 'rooms' of Embankment Gardens were given new bandstands, new seating areas and were opened up and made accessible to the street itself, connecting them with Villiers Street. We re-created the historic railings and lights of the Victorian era (taken from old photographs) enclosing the station entrance forecourt, creating an outside room for the Eleanor Cross monument. We made two arcades: one is a restored shopping arcade through one of the smaller arches; the other is a new, much longer arcade underneath Hungerford Bridge where Villiers Street exits to Northumberland Avenue and becomes the new river entrance to the area. All of these were out in the public domain, but there were also large internal rooms open to the public, such as the station concourse, in the larger arch the Players Theatre was reinstated and there is a coin market in one of the lower arches.

The temporary flat roof of 1906 was replaced by a large, suspended office building overhead, creating the new station concourse below it, a big room inspired by the great underground palaces of the Moscow and St Petersburg metros. The building is half a million square feet and sits above the station, like one of the great palaces neighbouring the river – the Savoy, Shell Mex House, Scotland Yard, the Palace of Westminster, Somerset House – all stride along the bank of the Thames. The office building paid for all the public realm improvements, including the new access route, the high-level public walkway that connects the original riverbank of the Strand to the South Bank and to Waterloo Station. The new pedestrian bridges either side of Hungerford Bridge were built very much in the planform concept as we proposed, but designed and executed by Alex Lifschutz.

We had an extraordinarily difficult challenge in creating the entrance office lobby to the new office building. At the Villiers Street level extending back into the building was a particularly long, large vault accessing the lifts which could only be on the far side of the train station where the wide platforms were. The length of the vaulted entrance lobby was considerable; there was a lot of noise from trains above and there was a problem with the excessive walking distance, but all of it was overcome by making it a spectacular interior. The noise of the trains was overcome by white noise, with fountains and waterfalls, some of them quite small with light features and dripping water. One of them was very large, like the canal features of the eighteenth-century French neoclassical architect Étienne-Louis Boullée. It was given a completely theatrical treatment so that it would become one of the great features of the whole office building. Of course all of this happens below the station level, so the office building has a railway station between it and its entrance hall, and therefore it combines major public rooms with the great private hallways of the office building and also an extraordinary complex three-dimensional spatial organisation.

We planned a similarly combined inside/outside urban planning project for the new Home Office headquarters building at Marsham Street (2000–05). The project replaced three towers which had been designed in the 1960s and 70s as the Department of Environment building. Both urbanistically and in their use of internal space, these three towers set on a podium were a failure and epitomized the 'building as object' of its time. The towers, very thin and twenty storeys high, intruded on views of the World Heritage Site of Westminster Abbey and Parliament and views of the river. They were so thin, so small in each floor plate and so separate from each other that interconnectivity between different sections of the Department of the Environment was extremely inefficient. The podium itself was an impermeable mass: it extended round all four sides of the site; in all aspects it was a built exemplar of a Corbusian urbanistic diagram. There was no pedestrian permeability to adjoining areas and the whole district suffered from this monolith; it was an extremely bad neighbour in what is a very varied and charming part of Victoria with its wonderful squares such as Thomas Archer's St John's Church in Smith Square (1728), and St John's Gardens. There is a mixture of residential buildings, TV studios, other offices and houses going back several centuries mixed with new ones – particularly the spectacular late-1920s social housing by Edwin Lutyens which is just two blocks away in Page Street. All this great mixture had this unusable, impenetrable, intrusive monolith in its midst.

We had demonstrated to the government at an earlier date that if the three buildings were replaced by one of equal area but only six or seven storeys in height, they could actually have the same amount of floor area of offices but also some additional housing, some shopping, some public squares and spaces, and some porosity, so that pedestrians could link through to connecting streets. So in the first instance this was an urbanistic approach to the design of office blocks, producing mixed use, mixed spaces, public spaces, pedestrian connectivity. When we were actually appointed to do the new Home Office in 2000, having won the PFI competition, we implemented the urban design re-plan by providing three low, linked office block elements with housing all along the north

side, and divided the three buildings to get two public pedestrian routes. We connected the three buildings by high-level glass bridges so that the site would have a high level of flexibility, whether as three office buildings or two or one, depending on government plans in the future.

Internally, such is the building's size (nearly 93,000 square metres overall), it became an interior 'urban planning' exercise. Each floor plate was potentially of considerable size and each of the three ground spaces had a doughnut plan with a large atrium. To connect all three, bridges ran between the buildings. The two sets of bridge links on each floor resembled a street on which all the public realm features of the office building's internal urbanism could reside. So there one finds all the meeting rooms, all the cafés, all the key points for staff meetings and mingling, copying machines – anything that is shared was placed in small spaces and modules and in little landscape features along the street, which was over 200 metres in length. This truly is the vital social feature of the whole internal urbanism. The linear street up the three atriums and each of the three have a different role. The middle atrium is more civic in character – it is the entrance atrium where the staff gather when there is a meeting of all the Home Office employees. Sometimes as many as 3,000 of them will gather here on the upper-level walkways and in the atrium at the base, with the Secretary of State addressing them about major policy affairs that affect the entire Home Office and its staff. Of the two other atriums, one has an internet café and the other has a restaurant for the staff. Below, in the middle atrium there is a staff sports/leisure centre and a social facility, so that there is a whole interplay of interior and exterior urbanism. The Home Office building is itself like a village within the village of Victoria: the urban village externally, the work village internally. At the Home Office, DEGW planned the office workspaces, and we designed the interior public realm, including all the fit-out for the streets and atriums.

Two other large masterplan schemes are included here. In the first, Greenwich Peninsula (1996 – present), the layout of the streets of our Masterplan curve to arrive at the bend of the peninsula, always at a right angle, so that each street is given a soft, gentle curve that takes its shape both from the dome and from the bend in the river. Consequently the buildings along it have a gentle curve and when we had the opportunity to design an office building within our own Masterplan, it was an opportunity to reflect the very large landscape of the estuary, the bend in the river and the peninsula into the plan of the building. The curve of the office

building responds to these soft, sweeping bends so that when you sit at a desk in the office building itself, you can see the gentle curves in all the workspaces, in all the positions, in all the corridors. The buildings were occupied by Transport for London and we designed all their interiors. The resulting large, open-plan office floor area sweeps in the shape of the masterplan to reflect the bend in the streets and the bend of the river. From chair to far horizon there is an integrated range of scales: urban interiors meet external urbanism meets regional planning.

At Regent's Place (2009) on the Euston Road we designed an office complex of three buildings similar to those at Greenwich Peninsula and a residential scheme where new streets, new ways of relating pedestrian routes and connections were reflected in the office buildings and the office entrances. So the layout of the office buildings, the reception areas, all took their key from the urban plan itself. It is a piece of exterior urban planning that influences the interior urban planning.

Another urbanistic office scheme is the Consulate and British Council buildings (1992–98), in Hong Kong, where the street frontage and the contorted shape and very steep slope of the site (one in four at some points) led us to create a village collection of forms with different entrances to different component parts of the government buildings, partly residential, partly educational and partly offices. The government offices element needed top security but the British Council with its library and teaching facility and its art and exhibition areas were very public. All of this created a building form with many entrances along a curved street frontage that is very unlike so much of Hong Kong – instead it's very British, very like a London street building set overseas. There is one central statement, with twin escalators set in the middle position to take visitors to the axis of each of the two buildings at either side. From the link in the centre, there is a gradual choreography of movement through and into the different elements of the composition, achieving both a sense of togetherness, as the buildings are linked, but there is also separateness as the internal function of the two buildings is so different and differently arranged and planned internally. We designed and fitted out both building interiors, including the selection of artwork.

Workspace that is rich in variety as any village or small city would be, has now become more normal in the modern workplace. Identity, fun, particularity and workspace as internal placemaking has succeeded and is a long way from the office as a machine for working in.

# Television Studios, Camden

This centre was built for TV-am, a new independent television company established under an IBA franchise to broadcast early morning 'breakfast' television programmes across Britain. The development of a building that could be used as a visual background for the media, and which captured the spirit of this new enterprise, was considered essential to the brief.

TV-am was scheduled to go on air two years from the time they became a franchise. It required a very fast track programme and the building was constructed with a design and build package to a construction budget of £4 million for 9,290 square metres.

Located in central London, backing onto the Regent's Park Union Canal – an element in Nash's original scheme for Regent's Park – the site faces onto Hawley Crescent. At the time of construction it was surrounded by small-scale commercial and industrial buildings, although revitalization of the area had started to take place, with the presence of a street market and an increasing number of small shops.

The brief called for the creation of two new television studios, associated technical and production areas, and all office, administrative and conference facilities. The new premises called for part new building and part conversion of an existing 1930s industrial garage, built on two floors with a large central void of irregular shape. This original garage building was at the back of the site on the canal bank; the various and more recent buildings that had been added along the street frontage were demolished to provide space for the studios and technical facilities and an access courtyard.

The front wall developed its own language, establishing a curve in response to the street. So did the rear wall, which had new windows inserted, the parapets were raised and the stepped and rough brickwork painted. The ends of the front wall, given prominence by the curve of the street, featured large-scale logos. All these elements together form the composite nature of the design and the detailed nature of the completed exterior.

Internally, the hospitality suite, staircase, and the converted existing bridge – the main elements of the space – are tied together by a very suitable 'storyline' (east/west, sunrise/sunset, news from all over the world). The hospitality suite becomes a Japanese temple, the staircase a Mesopotamian ziggurat, the bridge a Classical temple, and the cul-de-sac at the other end a far western desert with Dallas mirror-glass façade.

Inside the retained building the plinth was extended all around the existing central void at ground level. The grey-and-black glazed block plinth is vandal proof; above it the construction and colours are much lighter in colour and form, creating a vertical progression from dark/solid to light. For acoustic reasons no windows were possible in the front wall, which became an applied billboard fronting the studios immediately behind. Silver-coloured industrial metal sheeting in different profiles, interspersed with bands of colour suggesting sunrise (and taken from the station's own logo) clad the walls. Furniture and fittings were included in the construction package to be specially designed and purpose built.

As hoped, the building in use conveyed its media image: egg cups were used as prizes for viewers' quiz programmes, a computer-drafted abstract of the keystone introduces programmes, and the atrium, with its transformed bridge within the Mediterranean Garden, was frequently used as a backdrop to pop shows and interviews. The atrium had become, in effect, a third studio.

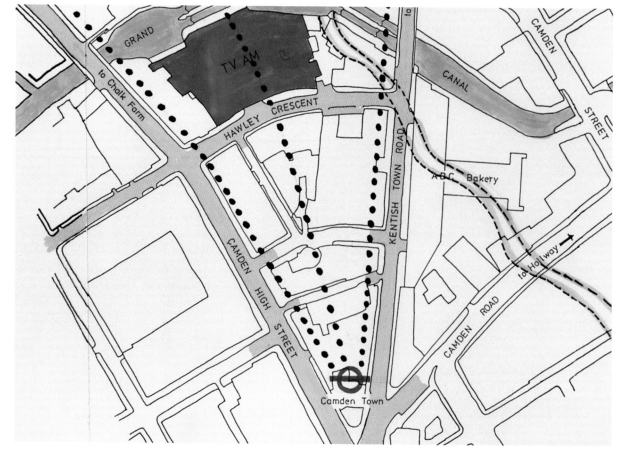

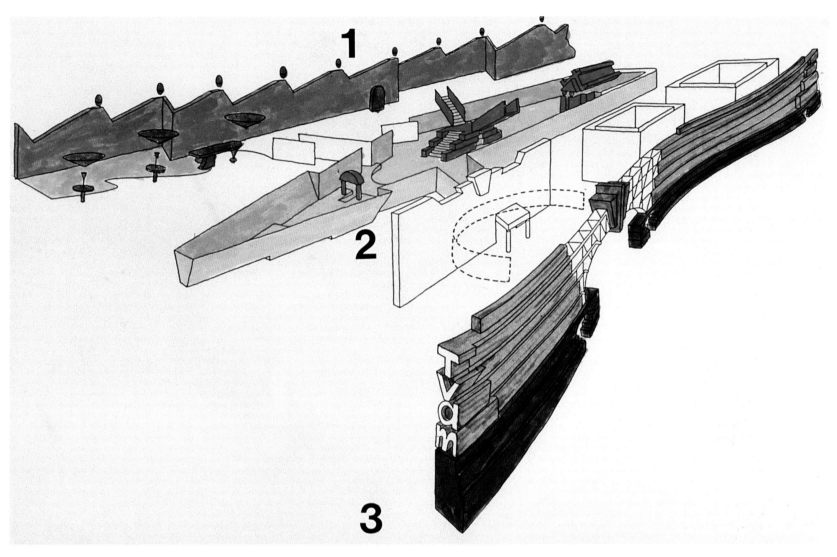

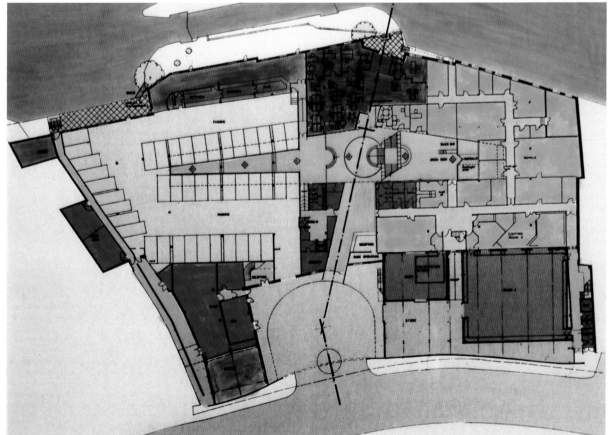

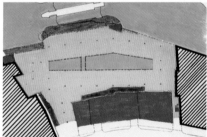

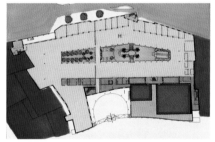

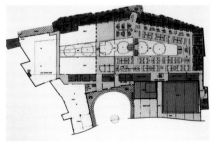

Top: Design elements 1) Rear (canal) façade 2) Middle atria and interior 3) Front (street) façade. Bottom left: Lower ground floor plan. Right: Strategic interventions and (bottom) ground floor plan.

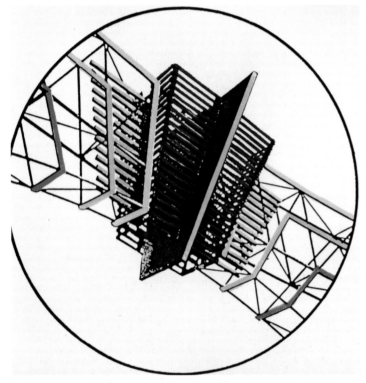

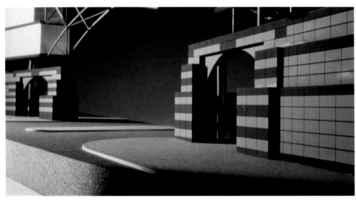

These pages: The building's exterior became a signpost and brand identity for its occupants.

This page: The eggcups became an iconic image for breakfast television – inspired by traditional classical urns, acorns and pineapples.

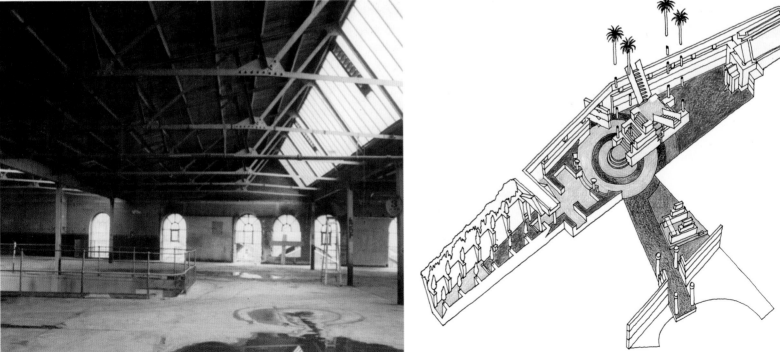

Bottom: The main interior space of the factory before conversion. Right: Axonometric sketch of central atrium ground floor. Top and opposite: The same space after conversion.

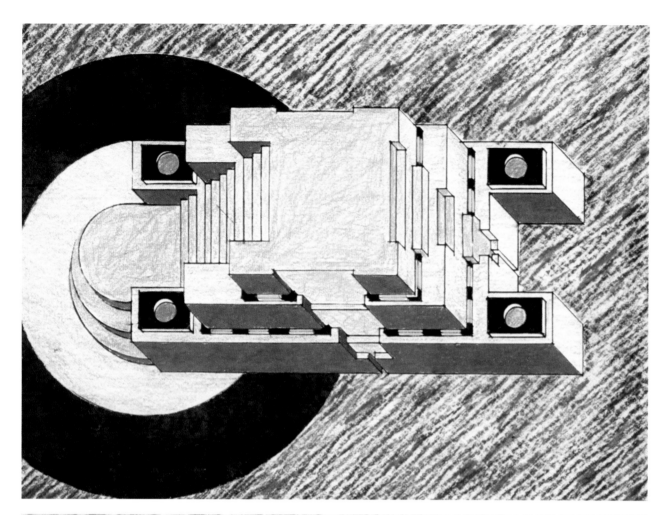

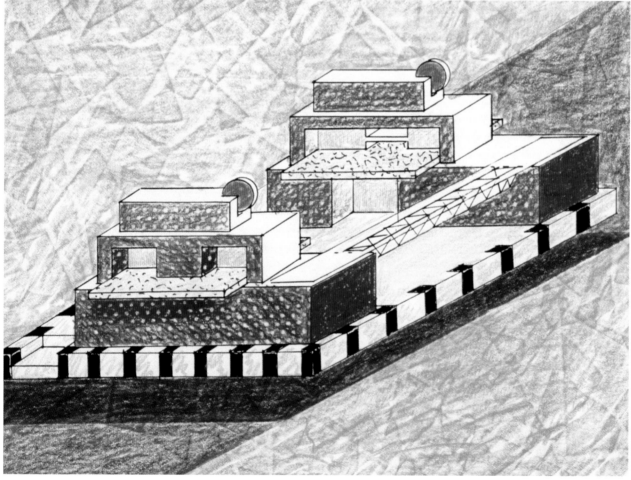

These pages: Interior sketches by Clive Wilkinson.

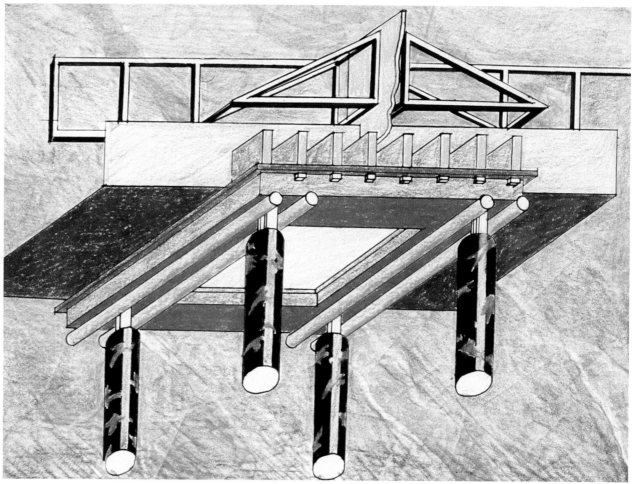

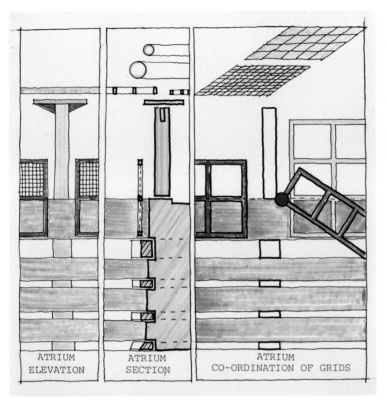

ATRIUM
ELEVATION

ATRIUM
SECTION

ATRIUM
CO-ORDINATION OF GRIDS

This page: Lighting and chairs designed by Farrells.

Top: The main atrium interior becomes an ad-hoc TV studio. Bottom: The main TV-am studio.

These pages: Furniture, light fittings and all detailing by the Farrells office.

# Television Studios, Isle of Dogs

Limehouse Studios sit in the heart of London's Docklands, an area that for a long time has suffered from the decline of London as a major shipping port. These studios were built for Limehouse Productions, a company founded as an independent technical and creative centre for the production of television programmes, both for established markets and the fast-growing independent sector. The location of the new production centre was strongly encouraged by the financial incentives offered due to the area's recent classification as an Enterprise Zone.

The scheme comprised a conversion and extension to a large 1952 warehouse, a three-storey brick-and-concrete-frame building of rugged simplicity. Two television studios were required, designed to very high technical specifications, with all the attendant production, office and workshop facilities. All of this was needed within a very short design and construction period.

The two studios were created by demolishing part of the existing concrete floors, walls and ceilings. A new mezzanine floor was added along the north entrance frontage to provide additional dressing rooms and related facilities. At ground level a large reception area acts as the main focus of the building, directing to the main stair and lift, the studios and production areas, and the public client rooms. Specially designed seating and a reception desk in the main entrance are constructed of laminate, cotton fabric and black and white marble.

Six major elements were added to the north elevation to provide additional accommodation and to give the building an identity, with obvious newly built elements. These are closely related in appearance and large in size; their scale links them to the massive bulk of the existing warehouse. To integrate the new internal spaces formed by these add-ons and to give external expression to key elements such as the main entrance, client suites, the star dressing rooms and the production manager's office, a 45-degree-angle geometry is used. They are constructed of vitreous enamelled steel panels in four colours, with plinths of glazed ceramic blocks.

The south and east elevations remain essentially as found, with the additions of an escape stair, an electricity sub-station and louvres, or solid infill panels, where required by internal constraints. The large plant room required by the complex servicing needs is situated at roof level.

Six large abstract bird shapes symbolize the building's waterside location and the spirit of communication.

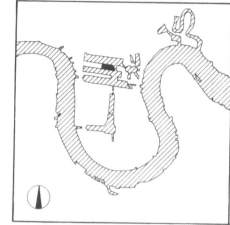

Location Plan: Isle of Dogs

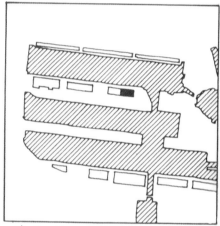

Site Plan: Canary Wharf

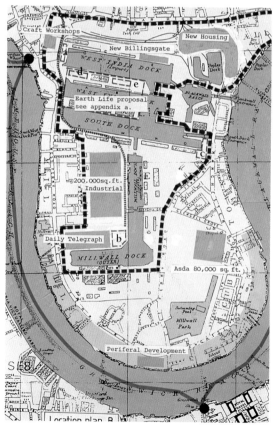

Bottom left: Early nineteenth-century development in the Isle of Dogs. Bottom right: Plan of Isle of Dogs before Canary Wharf.

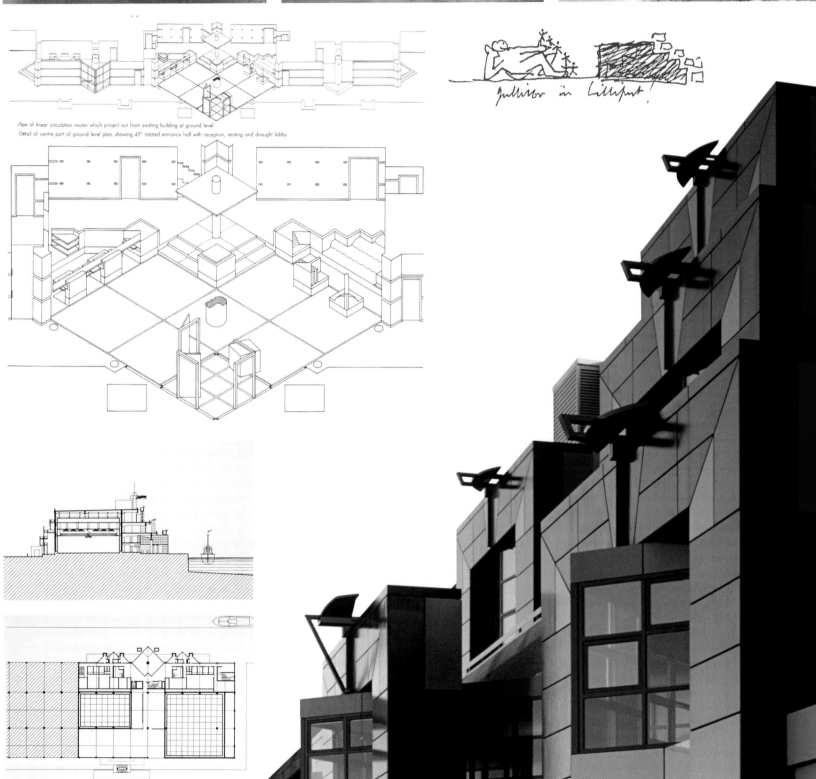

Plan of linear circulation routes which project out from existing building at ground level

Detail of centre part of ground level plan, showing 45° rotated entrance hall with reception, seating and draught lobby

Top row: Photos of existing building. Middle right: Terry Farrell concept sketch of adding components to the vast warehouse like Lilliputians on Gulliver.
Other images: Plans and photograph of the result.

This page: The entrance area was offset 45 degrees from the façade. Opposite: Furniture, wallpaper, lighting and all details were designed by the Farrells office.

These pages: Many of the furniture elements were specially designed. Bottom centre: The control rooms. Bottom left: The main studio.

These pages: Stairs and lobbies on the first floor.

# Offices & Urban Regeneration, Westminster

Embankment Place is a unique example of Farrell's ability to use urban design and planning to integrate major engineering and infrastructure in sensitive urban locations. This new office building is a major multidimensional development complex that uses the air rights over Charing Cross Station in a restored environment.

Charing Cross Station is London's most densely utilized terminus, so a major aspect of the design and construction of the project was to ensure that the functioning of the station was not impaired. The solution was to suspend the seven to nine storeys of offices above the tracks – a technologically innovative and ambitious structural approach which keeps the large-scale development isolated from railway vibration.

The air-rights building contains approximately 41,806 square metres gross of office accommodation. The entire structure is based on 18 columns, which rise through the station platforms to support the arch from which the office floors are suspended. Two atria penetrate the floor plates, and the principal cores (containing cloakrooms, toilets and escape staircases) are placed alongside the existing station walls on the building perimeter.

Retail and restaurant accommodation amounting to 2,787 square metres is distributed in the vaults below the station and in a new infill building, which completes the streetscape to the adjoining Villiers Street. A further area of retail has been inserted under the Hungerford Railway Bridge, framed by two new porticos that act as vehicular entrances to the development area, giving it a presence on the major thoroughfare of Northumberland Avenue.

The Players Theatre was moved to a new location while its essential character was protected within the environment of the arches below the station.

Environmental improvements under the masterplan were spread throughout the area, and included traffic management in Villiers Street and Embankment Place; the extension of the Hungerford Bridge to Villiers Street and onto the station concourse; and the enhancement of Embankment Gardens (including restoration and an improved setting for York Watergate).

A new platform environment was created below the air-rights building, developing the concept of the station platforms as a major 'room' and point of arrival. Changes to the station concourse were implemented, incorporating new accommodation for the train crews and staff. Improvements to the station forecourt included paving, replacement of the railings and re-establishing a fitting setting for the historical Eleanor's Cross monument, from which the station takes its name.

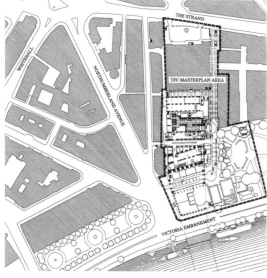

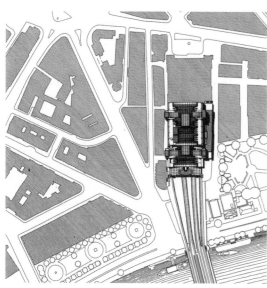

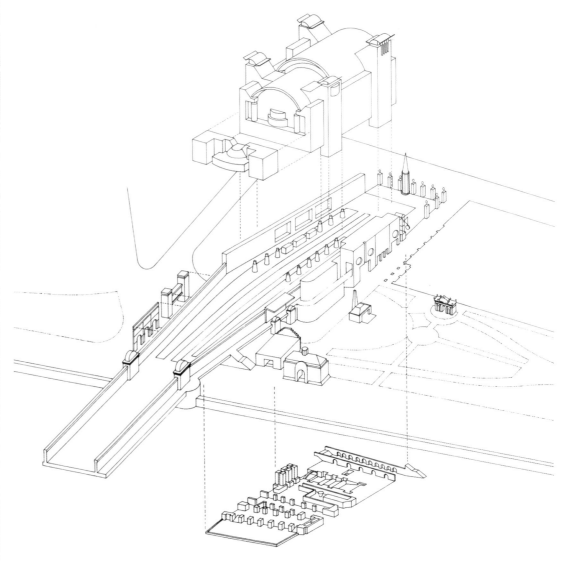

Top: View of the station from the South Bank. Bottom left and centre: Façade and balconies on Villiers Street. Bottom right: Detail of the river frontage.

Top left: Main atrium. Top and middle right: Details of the entrance hall fountain and seating. Bottom right: Plan of Level 1. Opposite: Main entrance.

Opposite and this page top left: Main entrance hall to offices. This page: New platform designs to rail station.

This page: Details of office entrance hall. Top: Ceiling lighting design in rail station. Opposite bottom: The reinstated Players Theatre in the arches.

# Architects' Offices, Paddington

In 1971, after the expansion of Farrell/Grimshaw Partnership and a long search for new premises, a late-nineteenth-century building with office use was found in Paddington Street. The interior, however, had to be substantially demolished and rebuilt to lay out the 315-square-metre offices over two floors. The two partners' offices, a secretary's office, the library and a conference area were located on the first floor, with the architectural staff and another conference area on the ground floor.

Herman Miller's 'Action Office' was selected for various furniture systems because of the wide variety of components available and the flexible layout it offered. The practice designed its own adjustable drawing boards, which adjusted onto the Action Office panels. Individual yellow pinboards were designed to match the wall lining, and upholstered Eames swivel armchairs were used throughout.

A suspended, overhead trunking system was designed to house telephone and power sources. The system was made up of 'Egatube' components: a lighting tray in the centre with PVC extruded industrial trunking either side. The cables were then brought down to each workstation through bright orange plastic tubes that clipped onto the furniture system.

After the split with Grimshaw, Terry Farrell transformed the high-tech office in Paddington Street into a richer experience. The intention was to develop the opportunities for spatial and visual character that lay beneath the bland surfaces. The use of colour and simplicity of spatial handling were replaced by complex spaces, richer surfaces and illusions that reused many of the existing elements. The Action Office furniture was reinstated but was integrated with panels, columns and an abundance of exotic plastic flora.

The long space was divided into five separate zones: a reception and conference area; staircase and corridor; architects' workstations; partners' office, incorporating a mezzanine library; and an open-air courtyard. The idea was to develop a central street with varied rooms and a courtyard – what Farrell called 'high-tech thinking with a friendly face'.

The reception became an art deco-style suite of armchairs on a complementary carpet and grouped around a fireplace. Marbled columns surmounted by spherical lamps culminated, in the infinite distance, in an archway – an illusion created by the calculated siting of mirrors along the rear and side walls. The courtyard recalled an artificial London beach, with bright blue wooden waves, rubber sand, a swinging hammock, lifebelt and beach chairs under a Martini umbrella.

A devout work-only environment had been replaced with colour and fun.

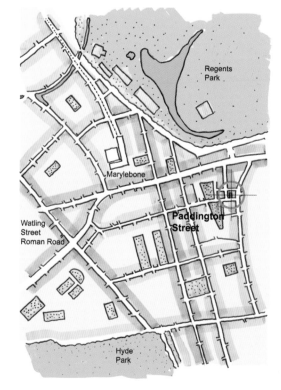

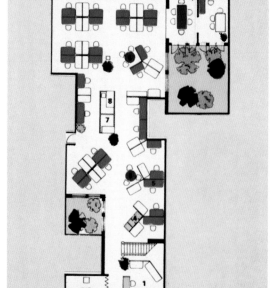

Top right: The first occupation 1972–80 by Farrell/Grimshaw Partnership. Bottom centre: The 1972 layout. Centre right and bottom right: Before and after conversion.

This page: The office's first incarnation, 1972.

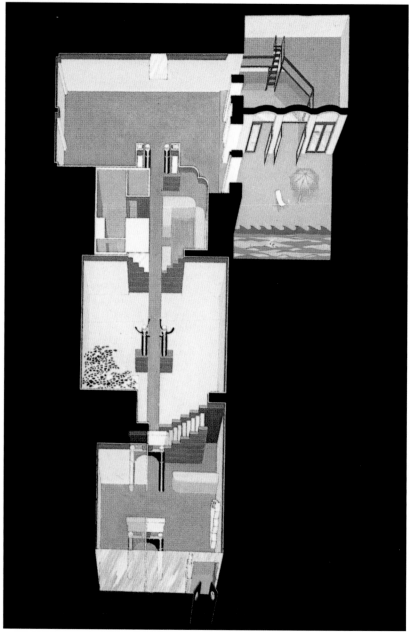

These pages: The annexe extension adapted in 1981. On revisiting later Grimshaw referred to this as an 'immoral use of Dexion [the metal structure]' – I liked that. In the background is a mock-up of panels for the Venice Biennale.

These pages: Revised office design, main street and staircase, after 1980.

This page: A monument from filing cabinets.

This page: Two further homes for TFP – top left, now Farrell's personal flat (see Homes chapter); bottom left and right are the current Farrells offices next door.

# Hospital & Consulting Suites, Marylebone

The London Clinic in Harley Street is one of the UK's longest established and largest independent hospitals. The masterplan comprised both new buildings and the extensive refurbishment of a listed mews building, which houses a new consulting and diagnostic house for consultants working in close association with the London Clinic.

The scheme was phased to enable an economic restructuring and expansion of the existing facilities whilst responding to the needs of a fully operational hospital. There were also sensitive issues concerning the conservation area and residential properties that adjoin the sites. First and foremost, though, the refurbishment was to be patient-focused.

The London Clinic facility includes 26 modern consulting suites, designed to facilitate the development of 'medical chambers' for groups of doctors with complementary areas of expertise within the same clinical specialty. These include gynaecology, urology, endocrinology/diabetes, orthopaedics, cardiology, and plastic and reconstructive surgery. To provide diagnostic and other clinical support to the consultant practices, there are X-ray, ultrasound, pharmacy and pathology departments located on site, while a broad range of outpatient facilities provide patients with a seamless one-stop service.

The quality and feel of the existing mews building has been combined with the latest technology to create a classic interior with reference to contemporary design. The refined detailing of the interiors complements the Georgian-style façade on Devonshire Place. Colours, finishes and artwork were carefully chosen throughout the building to contribute to patients' well-being and create a calm, familiar and reassuring environment. New glazed roofs bring natural daylight to the heart of the building and existing external light wells have been transformed into landscaped gardens. Within the design, care was taken to provide wayfinding for those unfamiliar with the building; all main circulation is visible from the entrance hall. Provision was made for disabled access via the new lift core, and each diagnostic department was designed as a self-contained unit to provide privacy for patients.

Extensive consultation with the hospital's clinical staff has resulted in a refurbishment which emphasizes the delivery of patient-focused care above all else. This has been achieved, along with a distinct character and a balance of functional, architectural and artistic quality.

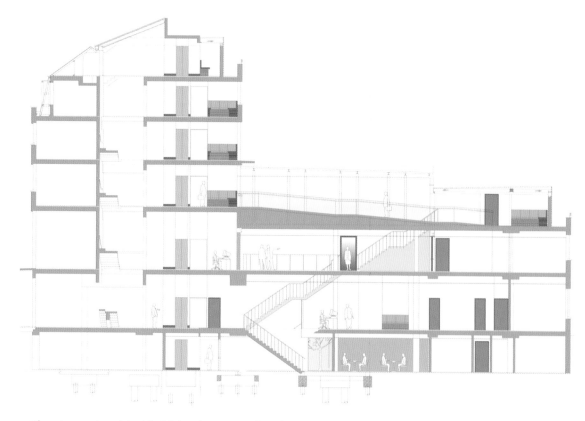

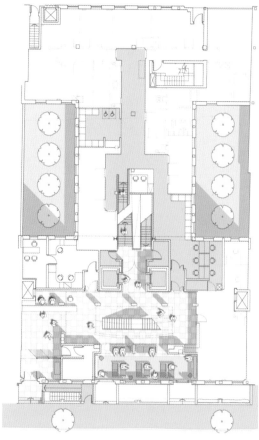

Three images top right: Model showing courtyard garden area. Bottom left: Cross-section. Bottom right: Ground floor plan.

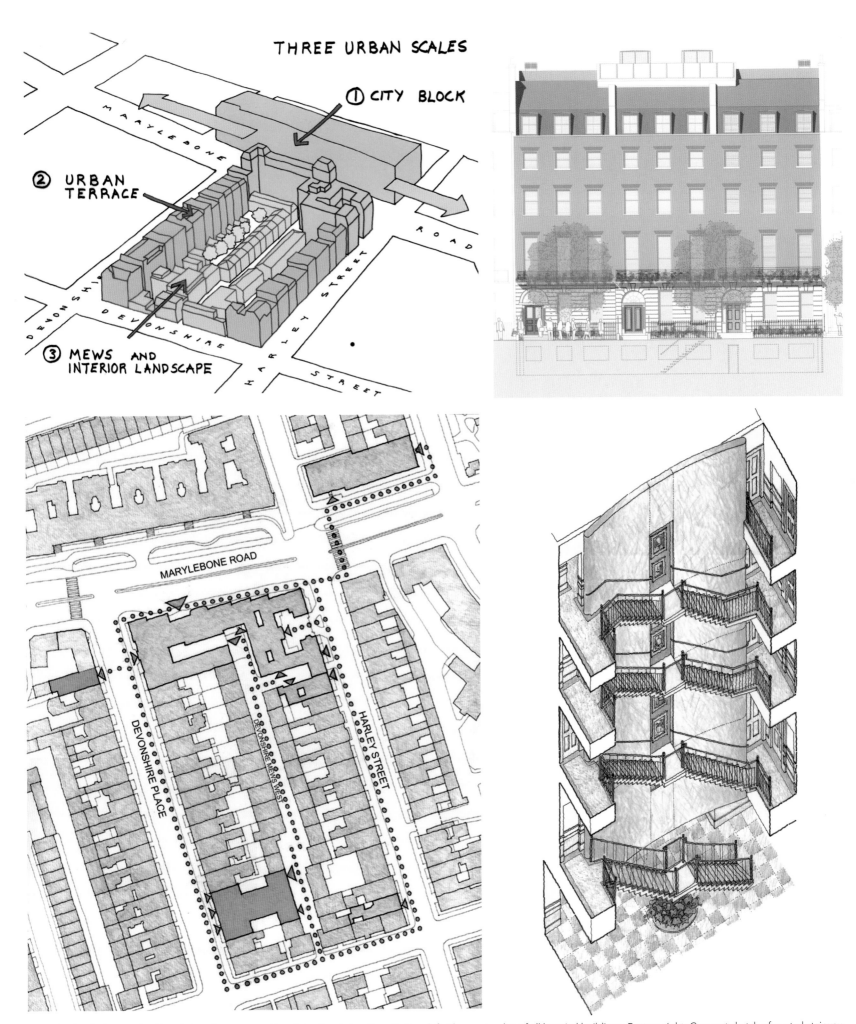

Top left: Sketch showing building in its urban context. Top right: Front elevation. Bottom left: The masterplan of all hospital buildings. Bottom right: Concept sketch of central stairway.

Opposite: Internally the new toplight staircase holds the planform focus on all floors. This page top: The new outdoor dining area.

# Government Department, Westminster

The new Home Office is located within an urban district of Westminster, a neighbour to schools, hospitals, housing and listed buildings. Its setting is quite distinct from Whitehall's monocultural environment, a highly specialized arena of state buildings that includes the Horseguards, the Banqueting Hall and the Palace of Westminster. The Marsham Street Towers were built between 1963 and 1971 at the scale of the Whitehall buildings, and they had been creating a negative impact on a World Heritage site for three decades.

TFP's proposals for the site demonstrated the feasibility of a low-rise, mixed-use scheme, with capacity for office, residential and retail accommodation, which would not interfere with the superb skyline views, an example of urban design leading architectural form.

Various architects submitted proposals for Marsham Street; however, TFP had been involved in the redevelopment of the site since 1991, when the practice had prepared outline masterplan principles for British Land. Farrells then fulfilled the aspirations of the original masterplan by their alternative use of the site.

In March 2000, TFP developed their 1998 proposal for its final submission, retaining the main features of the original scheme but with substantial improvements to the elevations and landscaping. The proposal focused on reinstating the area's historic pattern and addressing the restricted public circulation of the existing development. The aim was to create an inclusive, civic community and an enhanced public realm, coupled with high-quality architectural design.

At the centre of the masterplan there are three linked low-rise buildings comprising a central block and two 'bookend' pavilions linked by glazed bridges. These pavilions step down at the ends, allowing the central Marsham Street

elevation to relate in scale to the neighbouring Georgian terraces. The central block includes a public entrance, framed by a simple stone portico supported on stone piers and dignified by a five-storey-high glass screen and grand public space.

In contrast to the previous building, routes that give priority to pedestrians reflect Terry Farrell's belief that great towns include places where wheels come second to feet as a mode of transport. Three pocket parks within the site envelope create additional external space and pleasing views for office workers.

TFP's vision has been realized. The site boasts pedestrian connectivity, a tangible public realm with open spaces that encourage people to commune and communicate, mixed-use planning that promotes inclusiveness, and high-quality architectural design. Architectural innovation, combined with the resolution of urban design issues, offers a new community-orientated district.

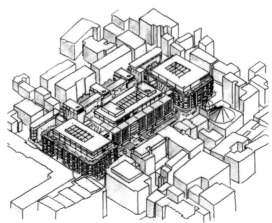

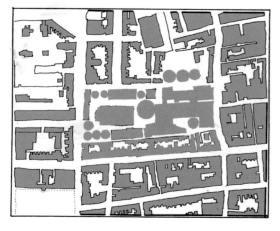

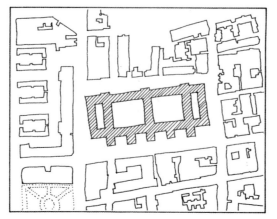

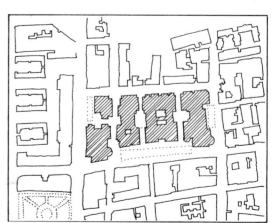

Top right: The original 1970s buildings before demolition. Middle: Masterplan proposal for the Home Office. Bottom left to right: Siteplans – early twentieth century, 1970s, 2005 built masterplan.

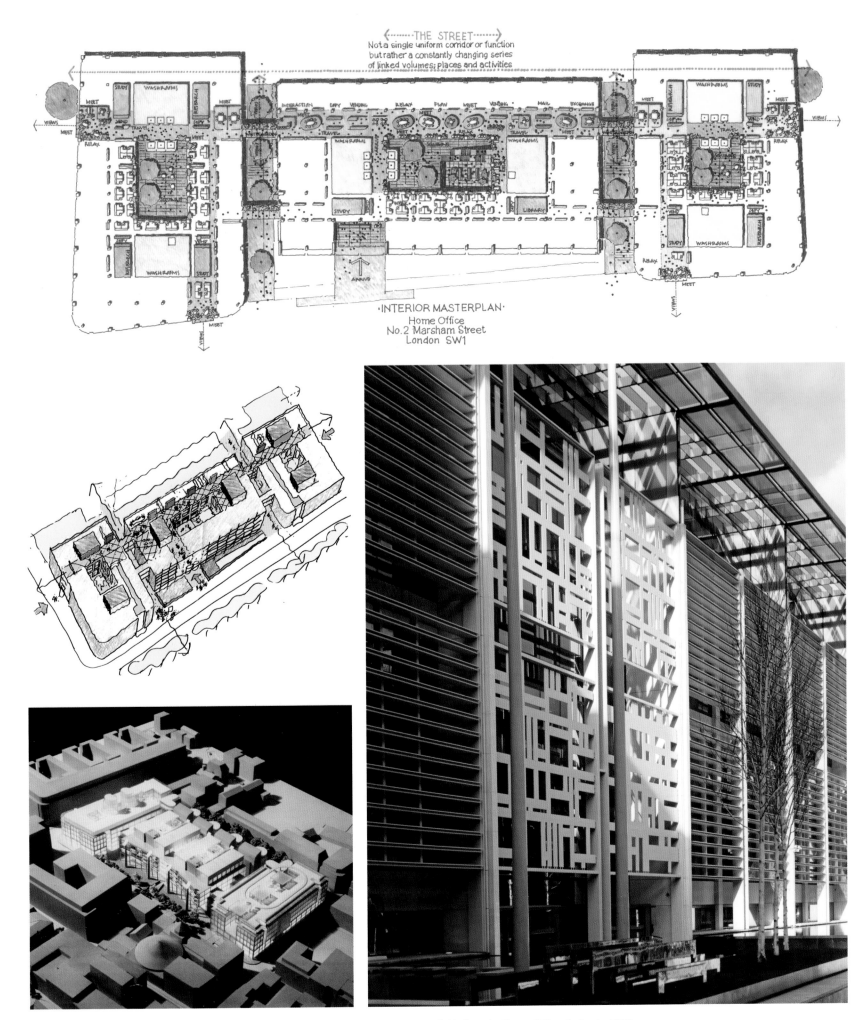

**THE STREET**
Not a single uniform corridor or function but rather a constantly changing series of linked volumes, places and activities

**INTERIOR MASTERPLAN**
Home Office
No.2 Marsham Street
London SW1

Top and centre left: The new internal street. Bottom left: The original urban concept model before the Home Office design in 1995.

This page: The main street connects all parts on all floors and houses 'public' facilities such as small meeting rooms and tea and coffee points.

This page: Main atrium with streets on various levels.

# Telecoms HQ, Paddington

Orange's London headquarters, The Point, was the first building completed at Paddington Basin, as part of a TFP 1996 masterplan.

Located on the western edge of the waterfront adjacent to Paddington Station, this flagship high-end office building was designed with two main entrances to accommodate different tenancy options, with a central bank of eight lifts, two of which are feature lifts within a glass atrium. The atrium incorporates ten hanging glass bridges, linking the lifts to the floorplates.

The massing of the building is a response to the site – essentially triangular, with two curved sides to the north and south, and two towers, with a recessed entry between, to the east. An external façade layer is 'wrapped' around the façade, incorporating the timber *brise-soleil* system to the south-west and becoming a light shelf as it moves round to the north.

The central concept for the fit-out is a volcano. The lower-ground floor is the 'magma chamber' of ideas, and the atrium the vertical focus of communication and activity, with ideas fountaining out into the wider world. This energy manifests on the outside with a ripple of colour up the centre of the entrance façade, culminating in a coloured glass sculpture at the top.

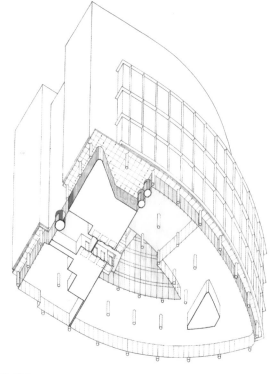

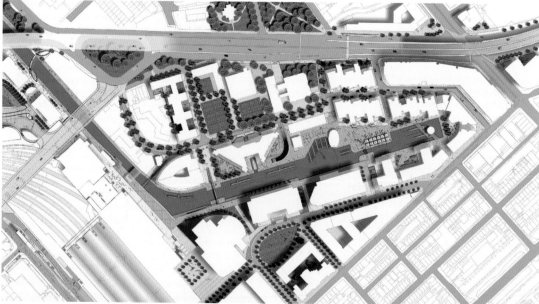

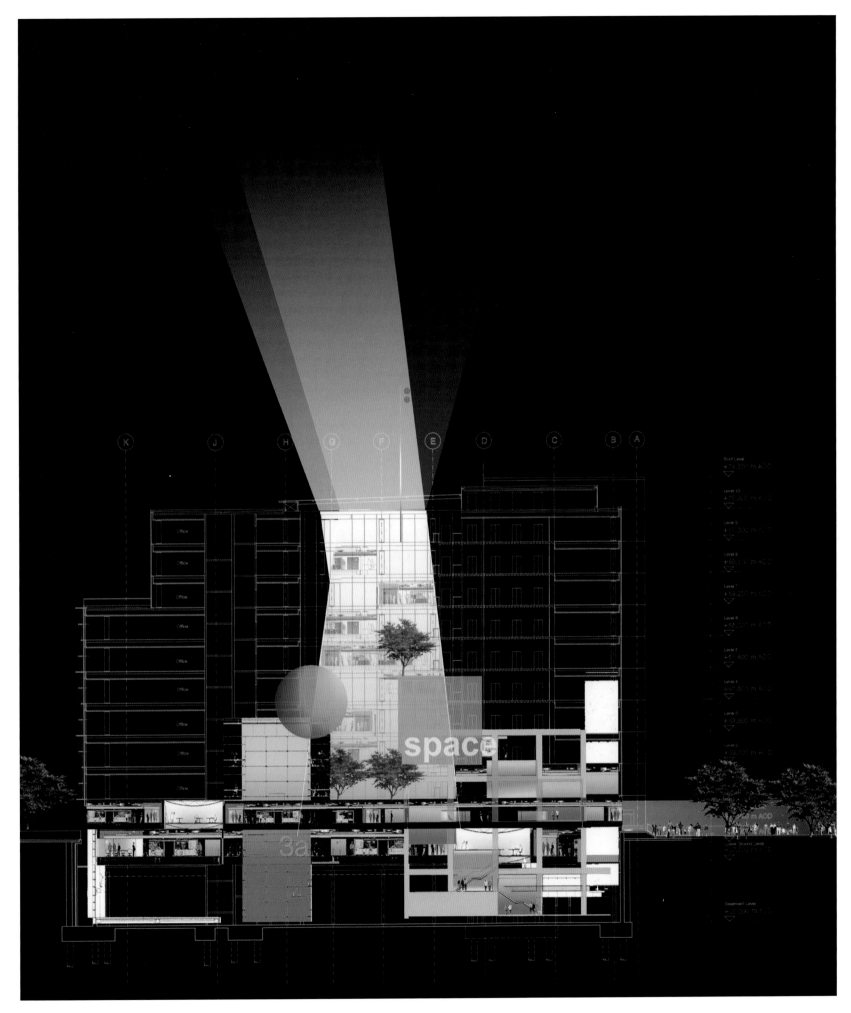

This page: TFP's winning concept design for the new Orange office interiors.

# Television Company, Westminster

The brief for Carlton Television Headquarters, in association with DEGW, was to house 600–700 staff and include corporate and business facilities, programme makers and sales departments, augmented by some broadcasting and scheduling services and post-production facilities, and a retail unit on the ground floor.

A major feature of the design is a 'street' that runs from the front to the back of the building at every level; all 'streets' are connected by a new accommodation staircase. The staircase reinforces the concept of the 'street' as a circulation spine, which is the focus of communal activities on each floor. The effect is an improvement in internal circulation and enhanced interaction between departments on separate floors.

At each level the 'street' contains a mix of central and ancillary support activities. The use of shared facilities – including vending and café areas, informal meeting spaces, photocopier/fax and postal points and telephone booths – contributes to the community feel of these areas. By extracting these non-desk-based activities from the office floor and concentrating them within the 'street', a more peaceful environment can be achieved in the open-plan seating areas away from the street.

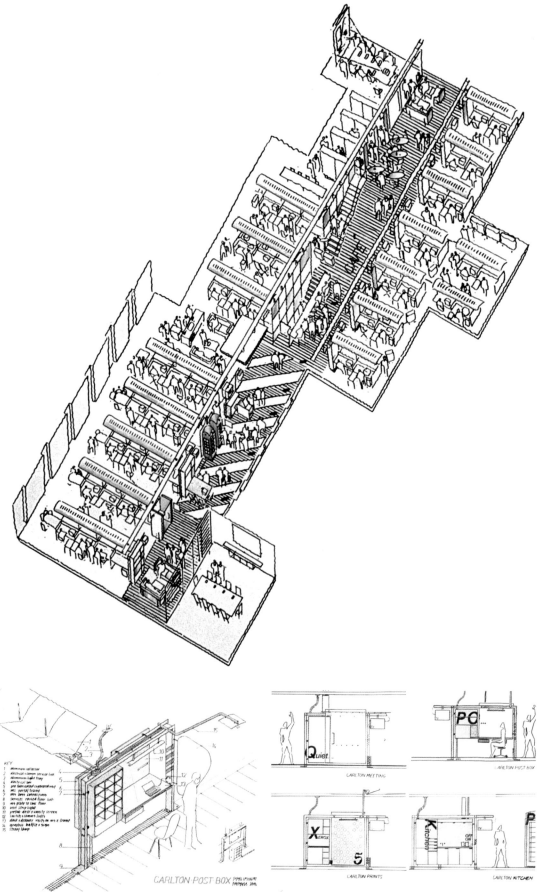

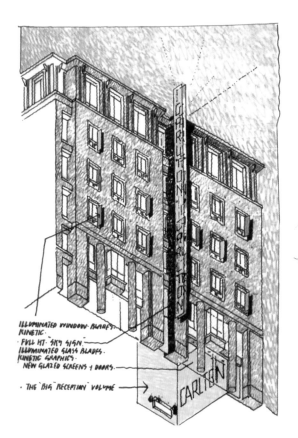

These pages: Sketches and details of external and workplace proposals.

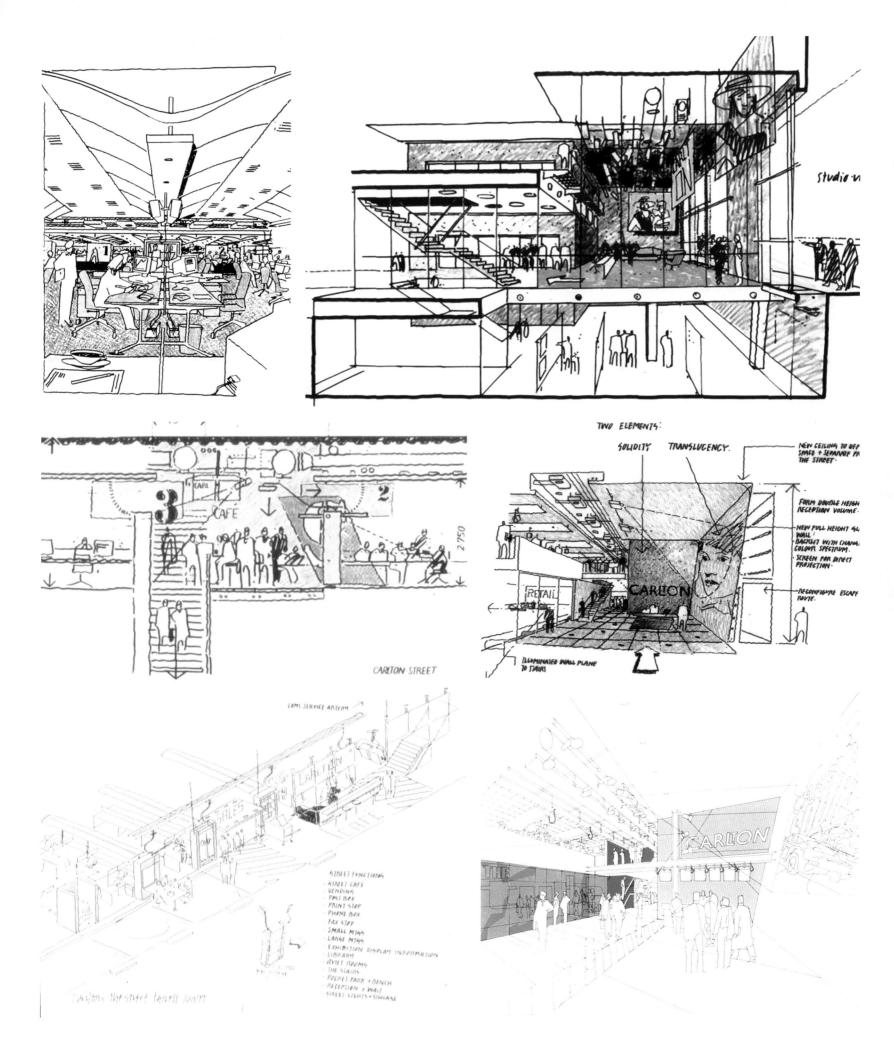

TWO ELEMENTS:

SOLIDITY    TRANSLUCENCY.

NEW CEILING TO DEF
SPACE + SEPARATE FR
THE STREET.

FORM DOUBLE HEIGH
RECEPTION VOLUME.

NEW FULL HEIGHT SL
WALL :
BACKLIT WITH CHANG
COLOUR SPECTRUM.
SCREEN FOR DIRECT
PROJECTION.

RECONFIGURE ESCAPE
ROUTE.

RETAIL    CARLTON

ILLUMINATED WALL PLANE
TO STAIRS

CARLTON STREET

COMS SERVICE ANTENN

STREET FUNCTIONS:
STREET CAFE
VENDING
POST BOX
PRINT STOP
PHONE BOX
FAX STOP
SMALL MTGS
LARGE MTGS
EXHIBITION DISPLAY INFORMATION
LIBRARY
QUIET ROOMS
THE STAIRS
POCKET PARK + BENCH
RECEPTION + WAIT
STREET LIGHTS + SIGNAGE

CARLTON

THE

# Office & Masterplan, Greenwich

This project site, set within the Greenwich Peninsula Masterplan, comprises two office buildings. Their strong visual presence addresses both Peninsula Square and the new Green Place to the south.

Taking its formal inspiration from the masterplan's geometry, the buildings' concept is of three sliding 'blades' of office accommodation plus a landscape 'lane' on the ground plane, which establishes a new public space separating the two buildings and creates a strong linear route across the site.

TFL's priority for the building was to create a healthy, aesthetically pleasing and efficient work environment for employees that respected their various needs. Colour guides the users' flow through the buildings and helps to define and indicate areas and their different uses. Bespoke interior landscaping with a carefully selected range of plants provides a method of cleansing the air of toxic gases emitted from office equipment.

The generic floor layout provides open-plan work spaces with provision for six cellular offices. Desks are arranged to benefit from maximum daylight. Close to the entrances to each floor there are two larger social areas; a wood floor and plasterboard ceiling with bespoke lighting differentiates these spaces from the main office area. The cafeteria is divided into three areas – a bar, a restaurant and a business area – and each of these is defined by its own lighting, plants, furniture and colours.

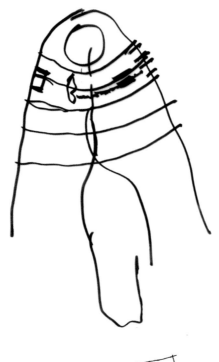

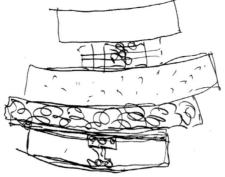

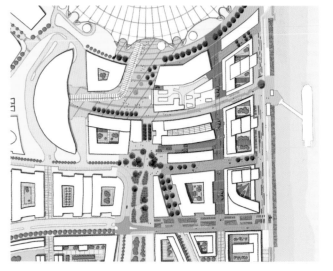

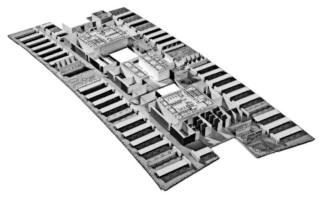

Top left: Farrell concept sketches showing how the buildings reflect the curved shape of the river bank. Top right: Masterplan model. Middle: Masterplan drawing. Bottom right: Single floor plate with office layout.

# Offices & Urban Masterplan, Camden

Farrells' masterplan for Regent's Place has resulted in a layout of buildings that creates a new and well-connected series of streets and spaces. It improves permeability and provides office workers and residents with direct access to the commerce, restaurants and shops to the south, and Regent's Park to the west. These new routes and more pedestrian-friendly hard and soft landscaping have transformed the area into a more coherent public space, which will gradually evolve into a new 'front door' for the west side of the entire Regent's Place quarter.

The development consists of two office buildings (10 and 20 Triton Street) plus a residential tower (One Osnaburgh Street). Number 20 Triton Street maintains a strong sense of identity while integrating with its context through material, colour and detail. The inclusion of the New Diorama Theatre within the building envelope adds to the social sustainability of the wider community – an amenity space can be hired for private functions, while the café-bar provides an active frontage and is a perfect backdrop for the weekly farmers' market in Triton Street.

The key interior space is the main entrance foyer. This double-height space opens fully to the street and provides a sight line across the new street and through to the internal courtyard. Soft-coloured stone is used throughout with dramatic vertical detailing to emphasize the space and provide dynamic shifts of light.

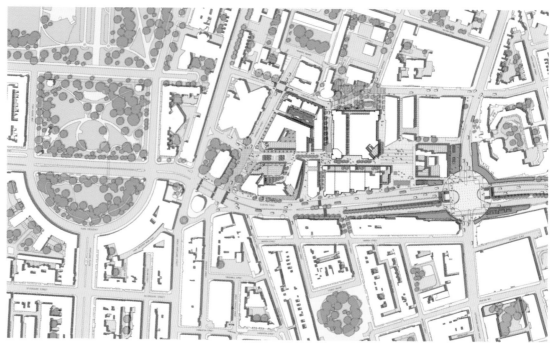

Top: Masterplan. Middle left: Osnaburgh Street elevation. Bottom left: Aerial view of development. Other images: Reception area of 20 Triton Street.

Top left and bottom row: Reception areas of 10 and 20 Triton Street. Top middle and right: Interior staircase in residential tower at 1 Osnaburgh Street.

# UK Government Complex, Hong Kong

Set on steeply sloping land next to Hong Kong Park in the Admiralty District, the headquarters of the British Consulate and British Council is intended to carve out a strong street presence. TFP felt that, while Hong Kong's vertiginous streetscape gave the city drama and vigour, the dissipated streets and ill-defined spaces had resulted in a neglect of spaces between buildings. The practice gave as much thought to urban design as to architectural design, ever mindful of weaving tradition and continuity into the urban scene.

To maintain separate identities, the consulate and council offices are housed in their own distinct buildings. The two headquarters buildings and the residential block create a long and continuously changing public street front to the north. The curved form of the complex means that its composition cannot be appreciated in its entirety from any one angle. From street level it appears to consist of independent buildings, although its unity is maintained by the roof and the consistency of materials. To the south, juxtaposed with the street elevation, lies a beautifully landscaped private garden.

The sloping site creates a processional route from the ground-floor entrance of each building that leads through the security area to reception and waiting areas. Internal public spaces of generous height and plan depth demonstrate another way in which the multilevel site has been used to advantage. While the same circulation diagram from entrance to lifts applies to all three buildings, the experience of the route is dramatically different in each building, exemplifying Terry Farrell's belief in the need for richness and diversity in architecture.

The design sets its own style and artistic integrity. Topped by a simple thin-edged flat-roof overhang, the elevations are composed of geometric forms rising from solid masonry bases that become lighter and more open as they rise – an effect achieved by increased areas of glazing. The palette of materials for the external elevations consists of Kirkstone slate, white and dark-grey granite, natural anodized aluminium and green-tinted glass on the front elevations, with render substituting the stonework on the garden elevations and residential block.

The building resolves itself through a complex interplay of opposites: open and closed spaces, solid and void, flat and sloping, public and private, urban bustle and natural tranquillity. Like the city itself, it is a building constantly in flux, providing a different face for each situation.

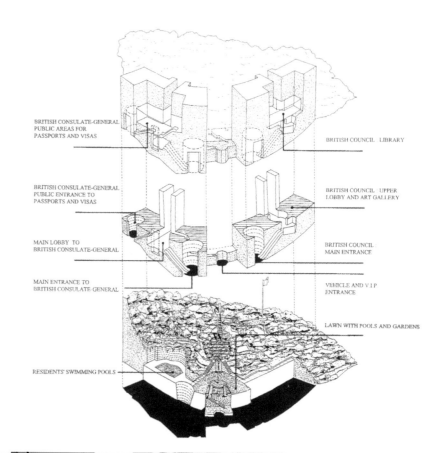

BRITISH CONSULATE-GENERAL PUBLIC AREAS FOR PASSPORTS AND VISAS

BRITISH COUNCIL : LIBRARY

BRITISH CONSULATE-GENERAL PUBLIC ENTRANCE TO PASSPORTS AND VISAS

BRITISH COUNCIL : UPPER LOBBY AND ART GALLERY

MAIN LOBBY TO BRITISH CONSULATE-GENERAL

BRITISH COUNCIL : MAIN ENTRANCE

MAIN ENTRANCE TO BRITISH CONSULATE-GENERAL

VEHICLE AND V.I.P ENTRANCE

LAWN WITH POOLS AND GARDENS

RESIDENTS' SWIMMING POOLS

Top: The choreography of street entrances and internal circulation. Bottom: View of combined main entrances.

Left: Entrance hall, Consulate. Right: Three views of British Council interiors.

'If (as the philosophers maintain) the city is like some large house, and the house is in turn like some small city, cannot the various parts of the house – atria, xysti, dining rooms, porticoes, and so on – be considered miniature buildings? Could anything be omitted from any of these, through inattention and neglect, without detracting from the dignity and worth of the work? The greatest care and attention, then, should be paid to studying these elements, which contribute to the whole work, so as to ensure that even the most insignificant parts appear to have been formed according to the rules of art.'

Leon Battista Alberti

Professor Tim Makower is a partner at Allies and Morrison, one of the UK's foremost practices in Architecture and Urban Design. He joined Allies and Morrison in 1990 having worked for the practice as a student since 1983 and having taken an internship in New York in 1987. He trained at the University of Cambridge and the Royal College of Art. He is the Co-Chair of Architecture and Urban Design at Qatar University.

The majority of his work relates to large-scale urban projects, a number of which are in the Middle East. In particular, he leads the work of the practice in Doha and Abu Dhabi. His work ranges from architectural schemes such as the Diwan Amiri Quarter and the Contemporary Urban Fereej's in Doha, Bankside 123, Liverpool One and St Andrew's Bow to urban planning projects such as the masterplans for King's Cross Central, London, Metrocentre Gateshead and Sidra Village in Doha.

Tim was the author of the Urban Design Guidelines for King's Cross Central and the Architectural Guidelines for the Heart of Doha, known as the Seven Steps.

He is the 'architectural voice' of Dohaland and has lead the development of a new language of Qatari architecture for their flagship urban regeneration project Musheireb. Having delivered numerous projects through to completion, both large and small, he is familiar with the maze of technical and political issues which have to be negotiated in order to realize an idea. He is driven by a belief that good design and the built environment can change people's lives for the better.

# Postmodernism and the Rebirth of Architectural Storytelling

**Professor Tim Makower**

The purpose of this essay is not to talk about architectural style. Instead it is about carved urban space and storytelling.

Storytelling? What kind of storytelling? By storytelling I mean the process – or perhaps I should say the habit – by which, in the hands of designers, buildings, groups of buildings and spaces between buildings communicate with each other and, most importantly, with people, over and above meeting the intrinsic needs of 'commodity, firmness and delight'. It is a habit that was not cherished or celebrated in the years between World War I and the late 1970s. In fact it was a habit, under the control of the architects and urbanists, of the Modern Movement, which had more or less died out.

The possibility that buildings and places and cities tell stories, or carry narratives, is an aspect of architecture that Postmodernism rekindled from a hearth almost gone cold. There are two kinds of narratives, which I am going to consider here. Firstly, I am going to talk about narratives of spaces, or places, and how façades can be used to mould indoor and outdoor rooms to give a consciously formed 'experiential structure' to the city; and how this can be a starting point for design rather than a by-product. Secondly, I will consider the narratives of architectural faces: how buildings look and how they can be understood by people, using their senses, their minds, their memories.

The reason for the modern movement, which began before World War I, is understandable. The natural economic and political process of enlargement, acceleration and formerly unimaginable enrichment which took place during the colonialism and industrialization of the nineteenth century changed everything for the makers of cities. Old cities became congested; beautiful neighbourhoods became slums. The motor car began to take over, and often it didn't fit. With immense powers across the globe trying to stake out their claims, compete with their neighbours or achieve security and stability, the world wars compounded the *tabula rasa*, the need for a fresh start.

We all like new things, and when old things are broken we have a choice: to repair or replace them. By 1918, the old order was certainly broken. The Modern Movement was a revolution and it sought to replace the old with something new but, perhaps on account of the extreme nature of the times, it generally refused to acknowledge the value of a tangible, and legible, connection with the past, and with existing context. It preferred to disconnect. Like all revolutions, the Modern Movement brought dogmas, and a tendency to oversimplify, which Postmodernism served to break and, thanks to that, we are all post-Postmodernists now.

In his seminal thesis *Complexity and Contradiction in Architecture*, first published in 1966, ten years before Postmodernism became self aware and gave itself a name, Robert Venturi (Terry Farrell's tutor at the University of Pennsylvania between 1962 and 1964) said of Modernism: 'As participants in a revolutionary movement, they acclaimed the newness of modern functions, ignoring their complications. In their role as reformers, they puritanically advocated the separation and exclusion of elements rather than the inclusion of various requirements and their juxtapositions.'

Before going any further I must thank Terry Farrell for reminding me of the timeless words from Alberti's *Ten Books* (Book 1, Chapter 9): '...as the philosophers maintain, the city is like some large house and the house is in turn like some small city...' Terry suggested that these words could be the starting point of this essay.

This statement, on face value, speaks of the continuity of experience, from the largest to the smallest scale; it implies a sense of proportion which holds all things in scaled and ordered relation to one another. It also speaks of the connectedness of inner and outer states, and of internal and external spaces. It reminds me of the importance placed by Renaissance humanists on achieving a healthy balance between the *vita activa* and the *vita contemplativa*.

To promote the interconnectedness of scales and spaces, inside and out, public and private, is fundamentally inclusive. Venturi, student of Alberti, warns that the Modernist revolutionary 'can exclude important considerations only at the risk of separating architecture from the experience of life'. I want to focus on the word 'experience' because it is here that we find the narrative.

Although Alberti goes on in his text to focus primarily on the city-like nature of the house and on the importance of appropriate scale and hierarchy in buildings, without dwelling on the house-like nature of cities, what is inherent in his words, nonetheless, is the notion of the 'outdoor room'. The idea of a public space as an outdoor room is common currency in our discussions of urban design and architecture today but it is easy to forget that through the Modern Movement, the city was seen more as a composition of objects – a still life – than as a composition of rooms, as in a house. On the other hand, Postmodernist urbanism reminded us, just as Alberti did, that the boundaries of human experience are essentially blurred; between hallways and streets, between lanes and piazzas, shops and courtyards, theatres and salons, bedrooms and balconies.

Let us go straight to the Palazzo Rucellai on Via della Vigna Nuova in Florence, built from 1446 to 1451 for Giovanni Rucellai and his family. Before looking at the elevation, its motifs and linguistics, it is useful to look at the plan. On this one instantly sees that the house is indeed a 'small city'. Although it was designed and built for one family at one time, and designed by one architect, its geometry is responsive, intuitive. Just as the city evolves over time, each development making its own responses to context in time and place, so too is the architect's pen responsive, moulding each room to achieve best fit with the awkward irregularities of this tightly constrained urban site.

But this is only the beginning of what this great work has to tell us. As with all the best architecture, its greatest qualities lie beyond itself. It is the formation of Piazza Rucellai and the modest but exceptionally important Loggia Rucellai on a site on the other side of the street which fully illustrates that the house and the city are a continuum and the boundaries between them are blurred. Alberti and his client have 'made a place' within the city by taking on the triangular block opposite and cutting it back, creating a space for the house to look out onto and, of course, from which to be seen. Furthermore, with the loggia designed as a meeting place for the family and the community, and as a private 'market place', they have created

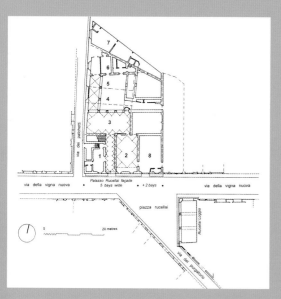

Left: Plan of Palazzo Rucellai and existing loggia showing internal subdivision of properties, after Preyer (1981) and Saalman (1988) (drawing by the author).

Middle: Paternoster Square and St. Paul's Cathedral. Previous development and Farrell, Beeby and Simpson Masterplan.

Bottom: Paternoster Square, urban form – Rocque's map, 1745; Ordnance survey map, 1873; Holford's plan, 1956; Farrell, Beeby and Simpson Masterplan, 1991.

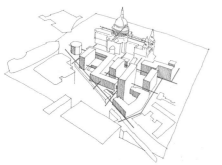
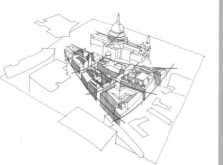

Previous development based on a rigid grid at right angles to the cathedral.

The Masterplan restores the traditional pattern of curving streets and lanes.

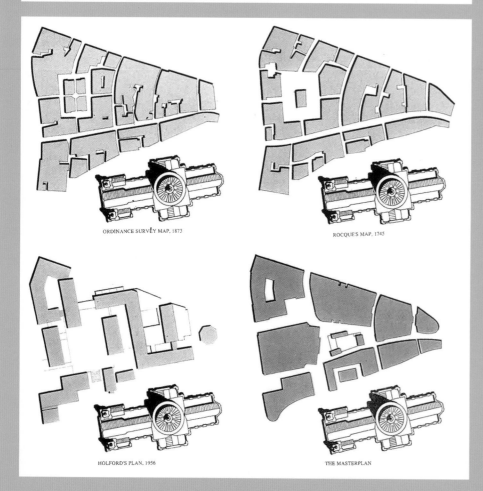
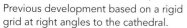

ORDINANCE SURVEY MAP, 1873

ROCQUE'S MAP, 1745

HOLFORD'S PLAN, 1956

THE MASTERPLAN

a focus for public life, under the aegis of a private name. To quote Franco Borsi in his *Leon Battista Alberti* (1977), 'it shows that Alberti made no distinction between the rational classical city and the city seen as a living organism.' This is not the language of the Modern Movement, and to be reminded of these things in recent years is something for which we can thank the Postmodern 'revolution'

For polarized approaches to the 'organic city', and a case where the Postmodernist approach came to the fore, there is no better example than London's Paternoster Square, by St Paul's Cathedral. We have only to compare Lord Holford's orthodox Modernist precinct, developed in the early 1950s, after the Blitz had damaged, but not entirely obliterated, this centuries-old portion of London, with the way it was before the war to see how carved space and storytelling were wrongly rejected. Holford's buildings, which I studied very closely as they were being demolished in 1999, were well-made, well-proportioned, well-resolved pieces

Apart from Holford's obvious urban design mistake – to create a raised podium which was not integrated with the surrounding context in terms of routes or levels – I believe the problem with Paternoster was that the buildings, individually and as a group, and the spaces between the buildings, spoke about nothing but themselves. The spaces between buildings are the resultant leftovers after rectilinear objects have been placed in space; the composition of form. In terms of the potential value of architectural storytelling, Holford's Paternoster failed on every count.

The spaces and the buildings surrounding them did not respond to the historic eccentricities of the City – for example, the angle of Newgate Street. They were not 'communicating'. They did not relate to the cathedral in terms of shape, alignment or scale (the fact that they followed its geometry seemed strangely irrelevant). There was too much space and the space lacked form. There were buildings but no urban blocks to form edges. The spaces between forms were sliced up, as were the internal spaces of the office boxes. The narrative connection which was missing here was twofold. Firstly, there was a missing link between the space of the square and the vast, exuberant volume of the cathedral; and between secondary spaces, large and small, indoor and outdoor. Secondly, there was no legible link between the site and its context, between the architectural language of these buildings and their surroundings, other than the use of Portland stone.

Thus this precinct of new buildings could not be read; it was alien, physically and culturally, both to the connoisseur of design and to 'Joe Public'. Why this failure? Because they were designed with their own intrinsic order foremost in the mind of the designer, rather than their context in terms of time, place and people.

By contrast, one only needs to look at the plan, especially the ground plan, of the Farrell, Beeby & Simpson proposal for Paternoster Square of 1991, to see a 'home-grown' narrative of outdoor rooms, treated as a continuum of spaces and places, large and small, interior and exterior; echoes of Alberti. We see the public spaces of this piece of city – the great interior of the cathedral and its theatrical piazza to the west front – connected in an informal but sequential composition to the new square, the lanes and the shops, the office lobbies and the public loggia. Most importantly, the masterplan gives containment to St Paul's, not in a geometric way but as a carved space; very much a recreation of the way it used to be; a simple retelling of a story from the past.

This masterplan came after a competition in which Arata Isozaki and Norman Foster made proposals which were just as alien as Holford's. Farrell, Beeby & Simpson were appointed, after the intervention of the Prince of Wales, to turn things upside down and explore, in Venturi's words 'the hybrid rather than pure'. They engaged in a narrative of informal place-making, treating the façades of flexible office spaces as they are; a backdrop to the city, performing a civic function. Without debating issues of architectural style, it is clear to me that one of the radical aspects of the plan was that it emphasized the character of the 'cathedral close' as a space resonant of the past, and achieved diversity and human scale by emulating the grain of the familiar streetscape of the surrounding city.

The original masterplan for Paternoster Square would never be classed as a first-rate piece of urbanism, even by Modernist standards, but it was typical of the vast influence which the giants of Modernism – particularly Le Corbusier and Mies van der Rohe – had on post-war Europe and America.

'Today I am accused of being a revolutionary. Yet I confess to having had only one master – the past; and only one discipline – the study of the past.' What did Le Corbusier, who made this paradoxical statement in *Precisions* in 1930, learn from the past? His sketch from *Vers un architecture* (1923) showing the pure forms intrinsic in the architecture of ancient Rome, reveals his deep-seated connection with the past, yet clearly illustrates his weakness as he

scales up from architecture to urban design. He sees the city as a composition of pure forms, a still life, and the urban spaces between the forms are residual. Objects placed in space cannot hold edges in the way that the best cities rely on for their spatial definition. Carved space, where urban edges are formed by the street façades of buildings, often touching each other, is a reliable format for cohesive urban space.

Why did the revolution of Modernism require, in so many cases, that elements were composed in free space on a grid? Was it a bid for purity or intellectual rigour? Was it an aesthetic of the plan which came more from the field of painting than architecture; almost a visual fashion, out with the old, in with the new? Was it a revolution for revolution's sake? One thing is for sure; it was indeed a break with the past and a trumpeted statement about the future being different. We know why a break was needed but did the baby have to be thrown out with the bathwater?

'For this was to be a city in which all authority was to be dissolved, all convention superceded; in which change was to be continuous and order, simultaneously, complete; in which the public realm, become superfluous, was to disappear and where the private realm, without further reason to excuse itself, was to emerge undisguised by the protection of a façade.' This is how Colin Rowe describes the Modernist city in the introduction to his seminal book *Collage City*, first published in 1978. It is a city of absolutes rather than relatives. It touches on the 'moral' overtones of the idea of a façade and by implication reminds us that storytelling was out of favour.

If Le Corbusier, student of the past, was a maximalist in terms of his architecture, loading his work with layer upon layer of content, Mies van der Rohe was quite the opposite. Where Colin Rowe attributes the dangerous cliché 'less is more' to Mies as his 'magnificent paradox', Robert Venturi boldly asserts 'more is not less'. However in terms of urban design, Mies and Le Corbusier are closer to one another and their works lack humanity in similar ways.

Venturi quotes Paul Rudolph's incisive words on Mies: 'All problems can never be solved... Indeed it is a characteristic of the twentieth century that architects are highly selective in determining which problems they want to solve. Mies, for instance, makes wonderful buildings only because he ignores many aspects of a building.' And that applied to his urbanism also. In direct opposition, Venturi's position is that, 'I speak of a complex and contradictory architecture based on the richness and ambiguity

of modern experience ... I welcome the problems and exploit the uncertainties.'

One of Venturi's 'complex problems' which Mies was not so much inclined to consider was the adaptation of the existing city fabric, and in one notable case he and Terry Farrell were pitched against each other. Farrell's scheme for Mansion House was designed specifically to be used at the public enquiry, to illustrate an alternative approach to Mies van der Rohe's proposal, designed for the developer Peter Palumbo. It was 1984 and London's architectural community rose up in support of the proposal, thinking it would be good for the city to have a building by Mies; good for its prestige as a centre of architectural excellence.

Mies' proposal was to cut back the 'flatiron' site, to create a rectangular site for a perfectly rectangular tower of 25 stories, to be placed on a single-storey plinth facing a rectangular plaza. In contrast to this, Farrell proposed the retention of most of the existing fabric, showing how a rich narrative could be woven into the site on the subject of established 'urban types'; types of space – the courtyard and the lane – and types of building – the chambers and the flatiron.

Not only can the two proposals be compared in terms of urban scale and richness but also in terms of 'characterization of place' and respect for history. If we imagine a sleek and slender box of steel and glass flown in from Chicago and dropped down in the City of London, how can it be anything other than generalizing in its influence; missing out on the associative power which architecture, new and old, can have in connecting people to their built environment; refusing to tell stories.

Looking at Farrell's scheme, again, it is the ground plan which is most telling. The main block is broken down into blocks of a smaller scale, permeated by routes, creating a courtyard in the interior of the block and blurring the boundaries between inside and outside; between public and private space. This form of urbanism is building on the existing narrative of the city's interconnecting spaces; using familiar urban types in a way which was, at that time, radical.

When the appeal failed, Palumbo turned to James Stirling, the architect who, like Farrell, moved from Modernism into Postmodernism at a midpoint in his career. Without getting caught up in a discussion about the perhaps overconfident architectural language of the 'Wurlitzer' (No 1 Poultry), it is a successful urban building and I am sure that it makes a more positive contribution to its context than Mies' tower would have done.

Although its colour, motifs and facial expression are in some ways alien to their

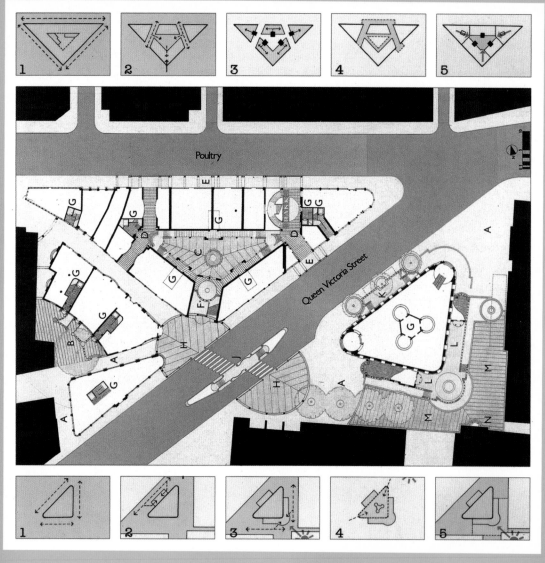

Poultry

Queen Victoria Street

Above: Farrell's Mansion House proposal. The Masterplan and concept studies.

Left: Postmodernism sketches (Tim Makower).

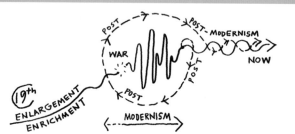

surroundings, it is a building which works with complexity, rather than denying it. It works with what is there and I would argue that this gives it a 'narrative' connection to its place and to people within that place. Both Stirling's and Mies' designs rely on simplification; both are strong statements. But where Mies' simplification process involves reduction, Stirling's involves synthesis – bringing together. More is more.

This is a building with a smile, a handshake; it steps out to greet the street, rather than just standing there being handsome. It is a building of uninhibited 'body language' and, whether I like its looks or not, its lack of inhibition is admirable, and deeply Postmodern. If there could be one unanimously agreed point coming from this essay, I would hope that it would be that the dogmas and inhibitions of the Modern Movement, those which demand that intrinsic order should prevail over extrinsic harmonies, are damaging to the making of the best cities.

Before moving onto the 'facial narrative' of architecture, let me take stock of the ground I have covered regarding 'spatial narrative' so far. Postmodernism reminded us that carved space, as opposed to the placement of free-standing objects, is an essential part of the toolkit for successful city-making. If architectural spaces are not treated as a continuum and conceived from an experiential point of view, inside and out, they will not hold together – they will not relate well to each other, to people or to surrounding context.

An uninhibited and inclusive approach to design is a good one. The pursuit of tidiness is generally less enriching than complexity. Although rich simplicity is a beautiful thing, it all too easily ends up as simpleness. Venturi was right in preferring 'black and white, and sometimes gray', to black or white.

Sebastiano Serlio in his well-known characterizations of the tragic and comic city, treats the buildings as actors in a play, as urban types who are wearing costumes. Together they form a space – more orderly in the case of the tragic, more higgledy piggledy in the case of the comic – and their façades are the backdrop; the faces contribute to the character of the spaces.

We have already looked at Palazzo Rucellai and the way it goes beyond itself to relate to its context, to form both a backdrop to the piazza and a face for the palace. But can its face be read? What would Alberti have said to that suggestion? I think he would have said that it speaks not only of its own intrinsic order, but also of associations, references and shared memories; of the archetype of a palace, and of course, of ancient Rome. These are old stories told in a new way. There are many nuances to the façade, the likes of which would be considered 'dishonest' by the Modern Movement. Most obviously, the fact that the divisions of the main façade do not correspond to the actual stone joints, which has fascinated architectural historians over the years.

What it reveals is a commitment to achieve Vitruvius' *venustas* (delight) without oversimplification. With a refreshing lack of inhibition, the façade has been designed to be 'read' at many levels. It acknowledges that human experience is made up of many layers, and shows that architectural language must be layered accordingly. It reminds us in a very human, indeed humanist, way that the integrity of a building relies just as much on its extrinsic relationships as on its intrinsic order. It is not that 'commodity' and 'firmness' are any less important than the Modern Movement stated them to be, but that if the challenge of achieving 'delight' in all its complexity is met with dogma rather than open-minded exploration, architecture will never fulfil its potential. Architectural reference may not be an essential component of all good architecture but it should at least not be outlawed. Meanwhile one would hope that positive human association, and the intangible sense of 'resonance' which we feel when architecture most pleases us, will always stand as a primary goal.

TV-am by Terry Farrell, covered in detail in this book, is a good example not only of the 'Shock of the Old' importance of certain seminal Postmodern projects in flushing out Modernist dogmas, but also of the use of a layered narrative in architecture.

The fact that a very new thing is created from an old warehouse is the opening line of the story; continuing the incremental evolution of the city, but not to the exclusion of a strong architectural statement. The extreme difference between the two fronts of the building continues the storyline. It rejoices in being the archetypal canal-side warehouse on one side and unapologetically shows its shiny 'I am a media building' front to the other. This is indeed the traditional way of urban buildings but here it is provocative, self-conscious, Postmodern.

The entry sequence is layered, from outdoor room – the forecourt – to entrance hall, and the threshold is blurred between interior and exterior. Inside, the highly specific atrium, with the qualities both of a courtyard and a grand hall, is surrounded by an industrial-style workspace, and forms the corollary of the exterior.

Meanwhile a literal, legible narrative is overlaid – another layer – covering the global influences of East and West (international media

catchment) in witty and conversational details. The memorable, and physically bold, use of the egg cup as a reference both to the architectural urn and the morning-time brand of TV-am sums up the accessible, uninhibited approach to communication which made Postmodernism so refreshing when it arrived.

Finally, a brief and revealing look at Embankment Place by Terry Farrell, another Postmodern icon. Its integrity in terms of 'commodity and firmness' is plain to see; it is a large floorplate office building spanning the platforms at Charing Cross Station. It forcefully fronts the river and its form and architectural language appear to be driven by the structural solution. But what makes this building philosophically different from, say, SOM's 201 Bishopsgate? Whatever it is, a nuance of architectural 'expression' is what makes Embankment Place postmodern. In every aspect – the large compositional moves and the fine details of the main frontage – there is a 'layer of language', which is referential-to-type, trying to connect this unusual air-rights building with its normative cousins and neighbours, the grand palaces fronting the Thames: Shell Mex, the Savoy, etc. Where SOM's building speaks about itself, Embankment Place speaks about its context in time and place. Furthermore, it explicitly speaks to people; it seems to be making an effort to mean something to the man on the street. The simplicity and strength of this statement as it faces the Thames is complemented by the extraordinary, complex, woven journey along Villiers Street at high level, connecting the station to Hungerford Bridge. It is a building of many layers, combining a rich urban narrative with the boldest of smiling faces. This could be called populism. It could be called storytelling.

Even if buildings are functional, technically integrated and good to look at, there is another layer; the intangible, emotional, associative (story-telling) layer, which I believe is a fundamental part of their potential, and of our potential as designers and appreciators of architecture. I have avoided using words such as 'metaphor' or 'symbol' to describe this layer because they are not open-ended enough; I prefer 'storytelling'. Architectural storytelling can be in one or many languages, abstract or figurative, loud or quiet; it can be more or less obvious or easily discernible, but it is a pity to deny that it exists.

As I read back over this essay, it seems odd that I haven't used the word 'minimalism' once until now. If we consider the interiority of the city as analogous with the interior of a house, then the way that individuals personalize their

own spaces, and the way interior space is prone to 'plenitude', can teach us lessons for how cities should be 'personalized' by communities. Designers have a role here – if not to deliver personal narratives, then at least to create frameworks in which narratives can thrive. A minimalist framework does not encourage personal plenitude, be it at the domestic or the urban scale, and Postmodernism reminded us that 'maximalism' can work.

Postmodernism has often been misunderstood as nothing more than an architectural style and, as such, it has been out of fashion. My intention in this essay has been to explore its more fundamental qualities. Its legacy is humanity, familiarity and personality in architecture and urban design. Postmodernism reminded us that there are layers of narrative on the agenda for architects and urban designers, which, if not employed, should at least not be denied. It is a shame if designers do not know or refuse to acknowledge this; it is a shame for the everyday inhabitant of the city.

Farrell has described Postmodernism as a 'flushing out' of Modernist inhibition. In as far as Postmodernism has reminded us of the outdoor room and its seamless connectivity with interior worlds, and of the idea that a building can display 'body language' and have a 'facial expression', and tell stories, and in as much as its quality does not need to reside in its being difficult to understand, it was indeed a successful revolution and, with expanded horizons, I believe it is something which all designers today have benefited from, whether they know it or not.

'One of the great strengths of the word ... "Post-Modernism" ... is that it is carefully suggestive about our having gone beyond the world-view of Modernism ... without specifying where we are going.'
(From a letter by Charles Jencks to *The Times*).

# Project Acknowledgements

There naturally were many who helped create the projects shown in this book. Rather than just list them alphabetically and attempt to include absolutely everyone (which would need another book!), I thought I would write a credit list based more upon roles and hopefully give some insight into the process behind.

On the personal Farrell family houses in Maida Vale and in Upwood, the co-creator that worked with me and for the long duration of the projects, was my then wife Sue and she deserves full recognition for her flair and her instinctive eye for colour and uninhibited expression. We had three builders – one-man bands as it were, who over 20 and more years followed us as we added, omitted and grew the houses – Eddie O'Brien, Jack Culbert and Peter Ashcroft. At the Hatton Street flat over the last ten years, Maggie Jones, my PA for over 40 years was in effect, the project manager and Rebecca Holmes in the last 3 years, the designer who helped me finish the project. On the Jencks House, of course Charles and Maggie Jencks were clients, collaborators and designers in their own right, and there were a surprising number of young architects in our office who were at some stage involved. Many went on to found their own practices, including Simon Hudspith, David Quigley, Richard Solomon, Simon Sturgis and Neil Porter.

On the Crafts Council, my then partner John Chatwin organized the project and John Langley and Clive Wilkinson were the principal designers. At the Dean Gallery, I had a really excellent client, Sir Timothy Clifford the then Director of the National Galleries of Scotland, who engaged creatively contributing many design ideas and was fully involved with the spirit of what we were trying to do. Duncan Whatmore in our Edinburgh office led the project up there and Dennis Dornan, Nigel Bidwell and Andy Bow were some of the designers, but many others were involved in the project.

At the RI, again we had a client, Baroness Susan Greenfield, who was forcefully and creatively engaged and drove the project forward with drive and ambition; without her, it simply would not have happened. The lead designer was Russ Hamilton (following on from Philip Smithies in the early stages) with Bea Young and Siggy Mepp and Neil Bennett organised all the tricky, behind-the-scenes affairs – planning, historic buildings, grants and funding, etc. Finally, in this section was the Great North Museum, which the RI team moved on to and Neil Bennett and Russ Hamilton continued with similar roles with Zoe Adeline and Sarah Lockwood, but I must particularly mention Casson Mann, who are really good, collaborative exhibition designers; on conservation matters we worked with the local practice of Purves Ash.

On the various workplaces, the projects were bigger and the list of architects, designers, project management teams seemingly endless; it takes whole armies to build a large urban office complex. Of particular note at TV-am: Joe Foges was the project leader, the design leaders were Simon Sturgis, Clive Wilkinson and John Letherland and Neil Bennett coordinated everything backstage, as it were; there was also Craig Downie, Alan Morris and Caroline Lwin. On Limehouse Studios John Chatwin was project leader, with John Langley, Clive Wilkinson, Oliver Richards and Laurence Bain. On TFP offices of course Nick Grimshaw was my partner in the first Paddington Street design and Geoffrey Smythe led the design team. On its 1980s remake, Joe Foges led, with Simon Sturgis and Doug Streeter the designers. Where we are now at Hatton Street, John Letherland, Steve Smith and Dennis Dornan were the lead designers on the different stages. On Charing Cross the overall lead at early stages was Neil Bennett, followed then by Susan Dawson and David Baynon and the overall lead designer was Simon Sturgis with Doug Streeter; David Binns did the Players Theatre interior.

The later office projects I can only summarize very briefly in the space available which is a bit unfair on the so many involved, but here goes: Russ Hamilton led on Regent's Place interiors, though the overall design team was led by John Letherland with Jeremy Boole and Karl James. At Peninsula Place the overall lead designer was Peter Barbalov with Brigitte Rothfuss interiors leader, and building delivery James Cregan. The Home Office went on over many years and has a big 'cast', but Mark Shirburne Davies organized and led on the final building, Aidan Potter and Doug Streeter were lead designers; interiors were led by Russ Hamilton. At 'The Point' in Paddington the interiors design lead was Aidan Potter and Giles Martin with Bobby Desai. On Carlton TV Aidan Potter was the lead designer. I should add that for many of these later office buildings Mike Stowell was our overall partner in charge and John Campbell our technical director for construction. On the British Consulate in Hong Kong Mike Stowell led with the designers being Richard Portchmouth (competition stage), Steve Smith, Paul Bell, Doug Streeter and Sue Farrell on artworks. On the London Clinic was Russ Hamilton and Aidan Potter with Chris Wade the overall leader.

Terry Farrell

# Picture Credits

Richard Bryant/arcaidimages.com: 5 top, 33, 34, 35, 36, 38, 39, 40, 41, 72, 73 top, 74, 75, 76, 77, 78 top, 79, 84 bottom left, 128 top row, bottom right, 129 top and bottom right, 130, 131 top, 134, 135, 136, 137, 138, 139, 141 bottom right, 142, 143, 144, 145, 146, 147, 170, 171

Casson Mann: 68 bottom, 116 bottom right

Graham Challifour: 78 bottom

Richard Cheatle: 14 bottom, 155 bottom

David Churchill: 84 top, middle left

Clarke Desai Architects: 14 top

Peter Cook: 181 top right, middle right, bottom right

Graeme Duncan: 80

Sean Gallagher: 168 top right

Chris Gascoigne: 181 left

Dennis Gilbert: 19 bottom right, 58 middle left, 149 bottom left and middle, 150 top right, middle, bottom left, 151, 153 top middle, bottom, 154 bottom middle and right, 155 top left and right, 172 top, bottom left and right

The Hancock Museum: 110 middle and bottom right

Andrew Haslam: 2, 5 middle, 59, 62, 63 top, bottom left and right, 64 top right, bottom left, 65, 96, 97 top row 2, 3, 4, middle, bottom left, bottom right, 98, 99, 100, 101, 103, 104, 105 all except bottom right, 107 top left and right, 110 top left, bottom left, 111, 112, 113 top left and right, bottom, 114 top and bottom, 115, 116 left, top right, 117, 118, 119, 176 bottom left, 177, 178 middle right, bottom middle and right, 179, 190, 192

Keith Hunter: 88 bottom right, 89, 90 bottom right, 93 bottom

© The Hunterian Museum at the Royal College of Surgeons: 68 middle

Athos Leece: 163 top left

J. E. Linden: 149 bottom right, 152, 153 top left

Steven Mayes: 110 top right

Derry Moore: 44 top, bottom left, 49, 51 bottom left and right, 52 top right, bottom left, 53

James Mortimer: 157 top left, 159, 160, 161, 162

Andrew Putler: 58 top right, bottom right, 61, 64 bottom right, 109 bottom right, 163 bottom left, 176 bottom right

David Read: 156 bottom right, 157 all except top left

Antonia Reeve: 87 top left, bottom, 92, 93 top left and right

Marcus Robinson 169 bottom right

Paul Rogers: 6

Sanders and Lund Photography: 97 top row 1, 102, 105 bottom right

Courtesy of the Trustees of the John Soane Museum – photo Martin Charles: 68 top

Tim Soar: 5 bottom, 23, 24, 25 top, 26, 27 top, 28 top right, bottom left and right, 29, 45, 46, 47 top, 48, 50, 51 top left, 52 top left, bottom right, 57, 58 top left, bottom left, 60, 64 top left, 85, 86, 87 top right, 88 top left, top right, middle, bottom left, 90 top left, top right, bottom left, 91, 163 right 3, 4, 166, 167, 189

Colin Wade: 180

Clive Wilkinson Architects. Photo: Benny Chan – Fotoworks 122 top, bottom left

Alan Williams: 150 top left, bottom right

Andrew Wood: 22, 27 bottom, 28 top left, top middle, 30, 31

Nigel Young: 149 top, 154 top, bottom left, 163 right 1, 2